# Critical Race Studies in Physical Education

Tara B. Blackshear, EdD
Towson University

Brian Culp, EdD
Kennesaw State University

LIBRARY OF
CONGRESS
SURPLUS
DUPLICATE

HUMAN KINETICS

SHAPE America

SOCIETY
OF HEALTH
AND PHYSICAL
EDUCATORS®

health. moves. minds.

## Library of Congress Cataloging-in-Publication Data

Names: Blackshear, Tara B., 1972- author. | Culp, Brian, 1976- author.
Title: Critical race studies in physical education / Tara B.
Blackshear, EdD, Towson University, Towson, Brian Culp, EdD, Kennesaw State University, Kennesaw.
Description: Champaign, IL : Human Kinetics, Inc., [2023] | Includes
  bibliographical references.
Identifiers: LCCN 2021043412 (print) | LCCN 2021043413 (ebook) | ISBN
  9781718212053 (paperback) | ISBN 9781718212060 (epub) | ISBN
  9781718212077 (pdf)
Subjects: LCSH: Physical education teachers--Training of. | African
  American youth--Education. | Culturally relevant pedagogy. | Academic
  achievement.
Classification: LCC GV363 .B53 2023  (print) | LCC GV363  (ebook) | DDC
  796.071--dc23
LC record available at https://lccn.loc.gov/2021043412
LC ebook record available at https://lccn.loc.gov/2021043413

ISBN: 978-1-7182-1205-3 (print)

Copyright © 2023 by Tara B. Blackshear and Brian Culp

Human Kinetics supports copyright. Copyright fuels scientific and artistic endeavor, encourages authors to create new works, and promotes free speech. Thank you for buying an authorized edition of this work and for complying with copyright laws by not reproducing, scanning, or distributing any part of it in any form without written permission from the publisher. You are supporting authors and allowing Human Kinetics to continue to publish works that increase the knowledge, enhance the performance, and improve the lives of people all over the world.

To report suspected copyright infringement of content published by Human Kinetics, contact us at **permissions@hkusa.com**. To request permission to legally reuse content published by Human Kinetics, please refer to the information at **https://US.HumanKinetics.com/pages/permissions-information**.

The web addresses cited in this text were current as of September 2021, unless otherwise noted.

**Acquisitions Editor:** Scott Wikgren; **Managing Editor:** Anna Lan Seaman; **SHAPE America Editor:** Thomas F. Lawson; **Copyeditor:** E before I Editing; **Permissions Manager:** Dalene Reeder; **Graphic Designer:** Dawn Sills; **Cover Designer:** Keri Evans; **Cover Design Specialist:** Susan Rothermel Allen; **Photograph (cover):** kali9/E+/Getty Images; **Photo Asset Manager:** Laura Fitch; **Photo Production Manager:** Jason Allen; **Senior Art Manager:** Kelly Hendren; **Illustrations:** © Human Kinetics, unless otherwise noted; **Printer:** Versa Press

Printed in the United States of America      10   9   8   7   6   5   4   3   2   1

The paper in this book is certified under a sustainable forestry program.

**Human Kinetics**
1607 N. Market Street
Champaign, IL 61820
USA

*United States and International*
Website: **US.HumanKinetics.com**
Email: info@hkusa.com
Phone: 1-800-747-4457

*Canada*
Website: **Canada.HumanKinetics.com**
Email: info@hkcanada.com

**SHAPE America - Society of Health and Physical Educators**
PO Box 225
Annapolis Junction, MD 20701
Website: **www.shapeamerica.org**
Phone: 1-800-213-7193                                              E8553

**Tell us what you think!**
Human Kinetics would love to hear what we
can do to improve the customer experience.
Use this QR code to take our brief survey.

# Contents

## Case Study 6: Black, Male, Queer, Athletic, and Academically Gifted 45

Challenging toxic masculinity, white supremacy, and stereotypes of Black sexuality

*Tara B. Blackshear, Afi C. Blackshear, and Akinyemi K. Blackshear*

## Case Study 7: More Than a Bathroom: Black Transgender Student 53

Black transgender girl (born male) locker room dilemma and disrespect by coach

*Tiffany Monique Quash*

## Case Study 8: PETE Candidates Are Ill-Equipped to Teach Students in Black Urban Environments 63

Student teachers grapple with accepting a job offer in an urban area

*Cara Grant*

## Conclusion 71

# Preface

## *Positionality of Race and an Intentional Focus on Black Youth*

Before beginning, we encourage you to take a moment to look at the image on the front cover. These are Black youth. They are unrestricted, ready to move, and engaged as they frolic through physical education under a rainbow of possibilities. We are led to believe by the image on the cover that the future is bright for these students and that their teachers are well equipped to provide a physical education that is empowering, transformative, inclusive, and life sustaining. The cover, like this book, is positioned intentionally as a reminder of what education should be for Black students. We are overdue in reckoning the inequities and structural hurdles that inflict violence on Black youth in schools and communities. Physical education is not absolved from critique, no matter how positively we perceive our subject matter. Unfortunately, the reality is that there are still groups who are denied full humanity in a nation that touts "life, liberty and the pursuit of happiness." As false beliefs about physical and racial differences persist and enact an immeasurable toll on Black people well into the 21st century, it is necessary to redress this tragedy.

In this book, we use the terms "Black" and "African American" interchangeably to reflect a social, political, and culturally constructed ethnic group identity affiliated with the African diaspora. The word "Black" is also capitalized to reflect this positionality. For Black people, the United States is a land of constriction, where policies of exclusion and suppression remain part of the fabric of American life. The permanence of structural racism and the lack of addressing this impact on our society in truthful and intentional ways is detrimental for all of us. However, a profession that seeks to "educate through the physical" while continuing to ignore Black students' experiences in a world obsessed with controlling their bodies is a profession that does not comprehend that teaching physical education in these times could be a matter of life and death for many Black students.

In 2020, it became personal. We decided to combine our collective experiences as licensed teachers, physical education teacher education (PETE) faculty, researchers, and advocates for diversity, equity, and inclusion in a collaboration to provide insight into the Black experience and physical education. This is not a new endeavor. Numerous scholars over the years have discussed the need for reforming curricula, reconsidering research and programming that frames Black youth through a deficit lens, eliminating instructional approaches that omit social justice frameworks, and improving teacher preparation and training, along with the need for organizations to end their commitment to neutrality on this topic. If the events of the past few years have taught us anything, they have underscored that America has a hard time talking about issues that have an impact on Black people with disparity and inequality.

As we have discussed elsewhere (Blackshear and Culp 2021), racism is a sickness that permeates every aspect of Black life, with deadly ramifications, as noted through research. From the time Black children enter preschool, they are expelled and suspended from schools two to six times as often as their white peers. Evidence of systemic bias in teacher expectations for African American students has been well documented over the past three decades. Exclusionary "hyper-disciplining" that targets Black youth in schools correlates with lower test scores, higher dropout rates, and increased exposure to the juvenile justice system. Personal stressors, untreated traumas, undiagnosed learning disabilities, instabilities in home life, and lack of safe spaces for play and recreation are recognizable characteristics of America's unsympathetic approach to the problems inflicted on Black youth. Thus, the work of improving social and educational equities for Black students is critical.

Although positive changes have emerged that increase opportunities for Black youth, their perspectives have generally been absent from PETE in a way that does not fully encapsulate the full spectrum of their experiences. Despite Black youth not living under the same Jim Crow laws that imposed significant political, social, and economic anguish on previous generations, their turmoil continues and is unique. Today's Black youth are navigating the systematic and institutional racism of the past, political capitalism undermining democracy, and law enforcement that treats Black bodies as a threat. Furthermore, Black youth are framed through media and technologies that provide content, tailored to white audiences, featuring Black pain, struggle, and death. Instead of providing real solutions to assist Black youth, time is spent traversing a cycle of emotionality where white people are captivated, stunned, repulsed, or rendered numb by guilt and the realization that the nation's history is not as pristine as they believed it to be. Indeed, there should be no wonder why slogans such as "We Shall Overcome," "Say It Loud, I'm Black, and I'm Proud," and "Black Lives Matter" exist. To be blunt, our nation repeatedly demonstrates that the lives of Black people are not valued. Paraphrasing from counseling literature, our obligation as professionals is "to know others as they are, and know them well," which helps frame the core understandings expressed throughout this book.

# Four Core Understandings

1. **We are in an anti-Black society that views Black bodies as expendable commodities.**

   Warren and Coles (2020) define anti-Blackness as "the socially constructed rendering of Black bodies as inhuman, disposable and inherently problematic" (383). Ross (2020) and Culp (2020b) further comment that anti-Blackness is present in laws and institutions that refuse to recognize the humanity of Black people. Anti-Blackness is a violent practice that is physical and psychological, and it is communicated to Black people through the suggestion of "norms of behavior" on how one should act in certain spaces. Over time, discrimination is normalized and becomes rules, regulations, and standards that are maintained and unchanged. While many of us have been exposed to an introductory understanding of racism and the struggle for Black civil rights, we are not presented with a complete historical view of how the Black body has come to be an expendable commodity (Yancy 2016). While this full perspective is not presented here, we need to explain some aspects of the journey.

   The institution of slavery in the United States set the precedent for Black people to be victims of unwarranted and cruel violence enacted toward them by white people (Dumas 2016; Yancy 2016). Slavery was enacted as an economic institution that is a recognized contributor to the building of America. This institution was championed by the self-appointed "founders" of the country—overwhelmingly, rich white landowners who perpetuated the social construction of race to their benefit (Dei 2017). Along with creating a hierarchy where Blacks were at the bottom of the human and class structure, the extermination of Afrocultural values, languages, and literacies occurred with various forms of physical and psychological torture to maintain whiteness and power (Dillard 2011; Sharpe 2016). Warren and Coles (2020) submit that this dehumanization created an American ethos that "views Black life primarily through the means of acquisition, possession, control, consumption, and destruction of Black bodies" (385).

   Previous commentaries on the ontology of the Black body expose implications for physical education, sport, and eliminating health disparities (Clark 2020; Clark, Smith, and Harrison 2014; Harrison and Clark 2016; Harrison and Belcher 2005). With respect to schooling, white landowners during chattel slavery prohibited academic learning because it would undermine the slaves' willingness to be subservient (Warren and Coles 2020). The definition of literacy has long been an area of contention because what "literacy" represents is little more than "white schooling," which commands dual control of the body and mind of Black youth (Delpit 2012; Dumas 2014). In discussing the need for the infusion of critical race theory in physical education, Clark (2020) espouses that schooling issues have stifled Black students and presented Eurocentric curriculum models that have taught them to "hate themselves." Along with the lack of explicit standards that provide successful pathways for Black students to succeed in physical education (Blackshear and Culp 2021), PETE programs have not significantly changed with respect to incorporating Black scholarship in coursework, faculty representation, and the overall routines of teacher education (Clark 2020; Hodge 2014).

Because sport and quality physical education are so heavily cross-promoted in schools, Black youth are still subjected to ever-evolving stereotypes and conceptions of their bodies. Within a white power structure, they are inescapably viewed as physically superior and intellectually deficient, and they are constantly under a white gaze, leaving other aspects of their identities marginalized (Clark, Smith, and Harrison 2014). Despite the representation of the Black body as strong, health disparities are rampant in the Black community. It is a paradox that positions Black people as unworthy of saving unless they can provide entertainment value to America through athletics or other creative and artistic means.

While anti-Blackness has undermined the futures of Black Americans, it has been particularly detrimental to Black girls and women. European beauty standards adopted across the world have long emphasized the image of a "proper woman" as being fair skinned, with straight hair, a thin nose, and lips, along with other anglicized features (Blackshear and Kilmon 2020; Bryant 2019). The result of these imposed criteria has long made Black girls and women targets of various assaults against their bodies, movement choices, and beliefs. This history is critical to grasping the viciousness of anti-Blackness in the forging of American identity.

2. **We must fully interrogate whiteness, curriculum, and the "racialization of space."**

Scholars in PETE have discoursed on the presence of *whiteness* in physical education and how it has influenced pedagogy, curriculum implementation, and assessment (Culp 2020b). Thus, for this book, it is appropriate to clarify this to better understand how spaces are racialized and used as sites to marginalize Black youth. To understand whiteness, one must remove the notion that the term is synonymous with "white people." As Du Bois (1920), Painter (2010), and Ignatiev (1995) noted, whiteness is a position of power and an identity supported by a combination of historical practices, laws, socially developed constructs on race, assumed group affiliations, and falsehoods. Dyer (1997) and Garner (2007) also provide additional perspectives to consider. *White* is the framing of a central position that serves as the dominant norm against which difference is measured. It "is the point from which judgments are made, about normality and abnormality, beauty and ugliness, civilization and barbarity" (34). Because of the dominance of Western European thought across the globe, prevalent in nearly every structure and institution, whiteness represents a "humanness, normality and universality" and not of a "certain race, but the human race" (Dyer 1997, 3). As Garner (2007) notes, positioning white as the human standard places a qualification on everything else, as anyone and anything not marked white is marked as deviant.

Because we are in a society that is erroneously touted as postracial, progressive, and unwelcoming of explicitly racist language in public, the workings of whiteness and the prevalence of white supremacy found in social, political, historical, institutional, and personal spaces can be hard to recognize when exhibited (Roediger 2002). Assumptions, messages, and practices have long been a pervasive influence in United States society and school curriculum (Ladson-Billings and Tate 1995). In schools, curriculum choices, lesson plans, and models for behavior have overrepresented the histories, values, perspectives, and accomplishments of the Western world and white Americans. Spring (2016) reminds us that history taught in schools consistently downplays violence perpetuated against Blacks and other non-white groups (e.g., colonization, slavery, lynching, policies). These master narratives center white people's dominance in American society while distorting, omitting, or even erasing the histories of non-white people (King 2014; Swartz 2009). The prevalence of the Eurocentric curriculum is a damaging prospect for non-white students. It communicates that there is an accepted racial hierarchy in which white students are preferred over everyone else. The subversive and conforming nature of the Eurocentric curriculum deculturalizes Black youth, undermines their self-esteem, and severely affects their desire for high achievement (Kunjufu 2012).

Like many of our peers, we have found that failure to provide an inclusive history of our country and the systemic racism in it has led to apathy toward the experience of Black people. Many of these dismissals have come from teachers, teacher trainees, administrators, and other organizational groups that promote physical education. While these attitudes can be found across different regions, socio-economic classes, income levels, education groups, and political affiliations (Dillard 2020), there is unique angst and displays of emotionality in discussing these topics with white people. The most pervasive that undermines the bulk of our initial conversations is the radical insistence on "colorblindness" and "impartiality." In theory, being colorblind is a noble intent. The ideals of colorblind practices reflect a world where skin color ceases to exist in favor of an equal opportunity for everyone. Indeed, many teachers feel that they will be effective irrespective of the student's background. We have been programmed to believe this through historical frameworks regarding teaching and learning. However, colorblind approaches are flawed, because they avoid discussions of racism and discrimination and promote the myth of meritocracy (Gallagher 2003).

As physical educators, we cannot allow impartial blindness to a world that routinely views Black youth as second-class citizens. Spaces for Black and non-white groups are considered, interpreted, and regulated differently than those of white people. Anderson (2015) reminds us that while the civil rights movement is long past, our communities are desperately segregated. He adds that society is still "replete with overwhelmingly white neighborhoods, restaurants, schools, universities, workplaces, churches and other associations, courthouses and cemeteries" (10). Despite the conceptualization of cities as accessible and multicultural, there are still areas that Black people are not expected to be in that are communicated in less formal, less direct, and less obvious ways (Harrison 2013). This "white space" is regarded as normal, unremarkable, and taken for granted by white people (Anderson 2015). In contrast, Black persons in these spaces routinely navigate through myriad systems, environments, protocols, and unwritten or assumed regulations tied to their movement and sheer existence.

When anonymous Black persons enter white spaces, they undergo an evaluation process where they are "sized up" to pass inspection by an arbitrator who holds power (Anderson 2015). If they are not authenticated, they could be profiled, challenged, interrogated, beleaguered, estranged, socially distanced, or killed. From minor to extreme cases, Black persons at the whim of a misinterpretation, bias, or intentional malicious action by the arbitrator experience physical or psychological harm. As a field, we have neglected the importance of teaching about how space is communicated and interpreted across different groups. Black youth live in a society where their bodies are under constant scrutiny and threat. Because issues of social status, class, and race are intertwined, physical education should teach critical topics related to space and distance. New perspectives and methods of instruction are needed to challenge long-standing beliefs on Black youth and perceptions of how they move in communities that do not fully appreciate them (Culp 2020b).

3. **Black students need empowering teaching practices to aid in their success.**

Black youth in 21st-century society face the covert reality that they live in a nation that consistently marginalizes the race into which they were born (Singleton 2013; Tatum 1997). Studies show that Black children are conceptualized in the social imagination of America as being older, reckless, and nonfeeling caricatures who do not need social protection or tenderness (Bernstein 2011; Carey 2019). As pertains to physical education, Black students have been viewed through a lens of athleticism, skill development, urbanism, management, and deficit instead of one highlighting existing community supports, excellence, achievement, resilience, and joy (Clark 2020). Unfortunately, this is an offset of larger issues in our educational system that has not fully valued the perspective and experiences of Black youth. Consequently, we need better narratives that incorporate a focus on deliberate, equity-centered policies and practices (Anderson 2016). These narratives should involve learning about the communities where Black youth live while expanding beyond the noble intents of multiculturalism and social-emotional learning to build meaningful connections.

Engagement in the community is a learned skill that requires assertiveness and intentionality. Physical education teachers would be well served by leaning on the wealth of knowledge and experience found in Black communities. As the demands of teaching have increased considerably over the past few decades, finding community support should be an essential task for teachers. The erroneous perception is that Black parents and community members are apathetic toward education. However, as Anderson (2016) notes:

> Education has always been of utmost importance to the Black community—from desegregating K-12 schools and colleges to establishing, managing, and maintaining historically Black colleges and universities (HBCUs), the African American community has always championed equality of opportunity and access for students because in this country, it has long been the key to social mobility and economic independence. (4)

With this in mind, what could this engagement look like?

First, teachers of all races must have knowledge of Black communities. In essence, they must work to understand the history of how Black communities came to be in the United States and are perceived to other communities. This involves learning about topics that have had an impact on Black mobility, such as desegregation, gentrification, and redlining. It also involves reflection on past and present demographics, recent shifts, socioeconomic makeup, and specific needs of students. Gaining knowledge of Black communities involves more than just looking at the data. Teachers must make it a point to listen to the stories of those who live in the community to help uncover factors (positive and negative) that affect students' lives. Knowledge of community is a strategy of learning that cannot be relegated merely to book reading, in-services, or professional development; rather, it is an active practice.

Second, non-Black teachers must work in advocacy efforts and be visible allies in Black communities. As physical educators, we tend to work on issues specific to the school environment. Nevertheless, health disparities disproportionately affect Black populations, and racism is still a noticeable deterrent that affects access to playgrounds and recreational spaces (Culp 2020a). Finding community partners who can work with your school, district, network, or program to provide capacity support, donations, or expertise is an opportunity to cultivate growth. Along with community members who can serve as cogenerators of knowledge, teachers should work to involve themselves in cooperative learning with other educators through communities of practice (Hausburg 2020).

We know that addressing the needs of Black youth in physical education means that teachers should use caution in exclusively highlighting approaches that promote multicultural and social-emotional learning. Multiculturalism is traditionally used to stress the importance of cultural diversity; the recognition of diverse ethnic, racial, and cultural groups; and the explicit valuing of this diversity in mainstream settings (Purdie-Vaughns and Walton 2011, 160). It is a positive framework for policies and practices that guide ideologies about how people should behave in diverse settings. Furthermore, multicultural approaches done well inspire self-esteem while emphasizing respect for people from diverse backgrounds (Banks 2016). Multiculturalist ideologies are certainly better than assimilationist or colorblind approaches. However, multicultural approaches are not appropriate in teaching Black students, for several reasons. First, they could increase stereotyping and subtyping by inadvertently leading people to categorize others. Second, youth could have intersecting identities that are not visible in their group identities, tied to class, gender, and sexuality. Third, structural inequality is real. In coining the term *diversity without oppression*, Andersen (1999) notes that multicultural approaches emphasize diversity without adequately addressing the ways that racial differences structure social life. Finally, multicultural strategies place African Americans in situations where they could invoke a colorblind approach to self-presentation in the world at the expense of feeling uncomfortable expressing their culture. Because multiculturalism is often preferred by well-meaning white teachers who want to project an "all lives matter" message to everyone, the approach is not only damaging to Black students but also to youth from other racial and ethnic groups.

Similarly, social-emotional learning (SEL) has an established history. SEL is an approach to human development that helps students in school develop techniques to cope with feelings of estrangement, isolation, and low self-worth while promoting high expectations and healthy identities (CASEL 2021). Ford (2020) mentions that educational professionals who have been trained in this approach can cause problems for Black youth and other children of color because of the culture-blind philosophy of SEL. She cites as examples the rise in hate crimes toward Black children and the racism prevalent in school policies that undermine Black students' success. Ford also asserts that SEL prevention and intervention methods must undergo evaluation to ensure that Black students are not dehumanized through culture-blindness. There is no way to work effectively in a "whole child" context when culture is ignored, trivialized, or discounted (Ford 2020). This sentiment is also expressed by Jagers (2016) and Simmons (2019), who advocate for SEL engagements that explicitly confront the impact of violence and white supremacy on students of color.

Given the persistence of anti-Blackness, teachers must work to develop meaningful connections with their students. In establishing connections, teachers should first eliminate two mentalities that tend to shape white teachers' thoughts about African American students—deficit mentality and the white savior mentality. The belief that African American students are deprived and deficient is one of the biggest problems facing relationships between white teachers and Black students (Ladson-Billings 2000). White teachers often hold lower expectations for the achievement of students of color than for white students (Sleeter 2008). These expectations have been informed by a history of racist assumptions and by research presented in books such as *The Bell Curve* that positions Black students as uneducable (Reyes 2019). In addition to the deficit mentality, white teachers might also engage in a "white savior" or "missionary" mentality (Hyland 2005; Matias and Liou 2015) that assumes that Black students need to be "saved" by their white culture and intellect. The persona of white person as savior has been advanced through U.S. media and is detrimental to the teacher and learner.

Successful teachers of Black youth are more than just good teachers. They get to know their students outside of the classroom, view them as extended family members, show curiosity about students' interests, and promote culturally relevant practices (Flory and McCaughtry 2011; Howard 2010). These teachers possess or seek intercultural experience in Black communities (Garmon 2005), are emotionally available, and understand that education must contain intrinsic connections to their culture (Ladson-Billings 2000). Furthermore, effective teachers of Black youth hold high expectations for student learning and can critically advocate for Black students in spaces where others misunderstand their life experiences, ways of looking at the world, and realities (Milner 2016).

Tomlinson (2002) provides five basic needs of students that we believe should be in the mindsets of teachers working with Black youth. These are (1) affirmation, understanding that students want to feel safe, cared for, listened to, and recognized as worthy of being in physical education; (2) contribution, allowing students to make a difference at school while helping each other in a cooperative journey of learning; (3) purpose, where students do significant learning that relates to them and has meaning; (4) power (or empowerment), meaning that students want to believe that they are capable of making choices that add to their success; and (5) challenge, where avenues are created where students can meet and exceed their ability, gaining a sense of accomplishment when they have completed a difficult task.

4. **We must adopt a social justice–oriented approach in physical education to assist Black youth.**

   The final core understanding of this book is that Black students benefit from teachers who apply a social justice lens to their pedagogical processes. In recent years there have been numerous calls for sustained attention to justice for marginalized and minoritized populations in physical education because such justice has been given scant attention in our field (Azzarito and Solomon 2005; Fitzpatrick and Santamaría 2015; Harrison and Clark 2016; Hodge 2014; Landi, Lynch, and Walton-Fisette 2020; Lynch, Sutherland, and Walton-Fisette 2020). The rationale for focusing on social justice in education has been of great debate since the 1970s. Those who do not believe in a social justice approach to teaching feel that it brings to the table unnecessary ideological viewpoints that infringe on First Amendment rights. Other critics espouse that the concept lacks a true objective and say that assessment is the only standard that should be measured in improving group outcomes. For some, the concept remains a buzzword that carries too much political risk to career employment and advancement (Culp 2016).

   What then is social justice? Although it is a commonly used term, there is no single universally accepted definition. However, Bell (2016) provides a definition of social justice that we will use here. Social justice is both a *goal* and a *process*. The goal of social justice is the full and accurate participation of people from diverse groups in a society that is mutually shaped to meet their needs. The process for obtaining the goal of social justice should be "democratic and participatory, respectful of human diversity in group differences, and inclusive and affirming of human agency at capacity for working collaboratively with others to create change" (34).

   Bell espouses that the vision for social justice is a world in which the distribution of resources is equitable and ecologically sustainable, where all members are secure, physically and psychologically safe, recognized, and treated with respect. Individuals are both self-determining, with the ability to develop their full capacities, and independent, with the capability to interact democratically with others (Freire 1970). Social justice "involves social actors who have a sense of their own agency as well as a sense of their social responsibility toward and with others in the society, environment, and broader world in which we live" (34). As such, teaching for social justice is an orchestrated task that requires an appreciation of the past and understanding of current events that affect teaching and the acquisition of knowledge to connect information while delivering content to help students (Robinson and Randall 2016; Walton-Fisette, Sutherland, and Hill 2019).

This definition is an important one to conceptualize, particularly as the term *social justice* has been co-opted and politicized to divert from its aims. Equally disconcerting is the lack of nuance between what constitutes justice versus social justice. At the risk of oversimplifying the two, justice is a want, while social justice is a need. In theory, everyone should be afforded equal justice, but the history of discrimination and bias in our society has shown that justice is not always equally applied. Social justice acknowledges that there are entities, systems, institutions, regulations, and historical practices that undermine the ability of an individual to have full participation in society. Merely saying that something should be promised does not mean that it will be. This is the conundrum that social justice attempts to rectify. As educators, we must acknowledge that we do not know everything, and we should be in constant reflection on issues that frequently change. Harrison and Clark (2016) remind us that true efforts in social justice involve a critical analysis of oppression and privilege that can help address inequities in education, physical activity, and health.

# Conclusion

Before moving forward, we want to lay out the original impulse behind this book. While we believe that other minoritized groups' experiences are important to understand, current physical education approaches to teaching do not sufficiently address the diverse issues Black youth face today. Black groups (particularly African Americans) have been subjected to unique discriminations, racism, and ongoing structural disadvantages that have affected their mobility and positionality in the United States. Physical education teachers who understand these factors and strategize for the success of Black youth increase opportunities that have a positive impact on their life success. Along with intentional planning and sustained commitment to this population, we know that establishing a classroom climate where all feel empowered to think, change, and act is achievable.

## References and Suggested Resources

Andersen, Margaret L. 1999. "The Fiction of 'Diversity Without Oppression.'" In *Critical Ethnicity: Countering the Waves of Identity Politics*, edited by Robert H. Tai and Mary L. Kenyatta, 5-20. Oxford, England: Rowman & Littlefield.

Anderson, Elijah. 2015. "The White Space." *Sociology of Race and Ethnicity* 1 (1): 10-21. https://doi.org/10.1177/2332649214561306.

Anderson, Meredith B.L. 2016. *Building Better Narratives in Black Education*. Washington, DC: UNCF.

Azzarito, Laura, and Melinda A. Solomon. 2005. "A Reconceptualisation of Physical Education: The Intersection of Gender/Race/Social Class." *Sport, Education and Society* 10 (1): 25-47. https://doi.org/10.1080/135733205200028794.

Bernstein, Eric R. 2011. "Listening to the Stories of Black Students About Race and Disciplinary Interactions With Teachers." PhD diss., University of Pennsylvania, 2011. https://repository.upenn.edu/dissertations/AAI3475829.

Banks, James A. 2016. *Cultural Diversity and Education: Foundations, Curriculum, and Teaching*. 6th ed. New York: Routledge.

Bell, Lee Anne. 2016. "Theoretical Foundations for Social Justice Education." In *Teaching for Diversity and Social Justice*, edited by Maurine Adams, Lee Anne Bell, Diane J. Goodman, and Khyati Y. Joshi, 3-26. New York: Routledge.

Blackshear, Tara B., and Brian Culp. 2021. "Transforming PETE's Initial Standards: Ensuring Social Justice for Black Students in Physical Education." *Quest* 73 (1): 22-44. https://doi.org/10.1080/00336297.2020.1838305.

Blackshear, Tara B., and Kelsey Kilmon. 2020. "Natural Hair: A Vital Component to Black Women's Health." *Journal of Racial and Ethnic Health Disparities*. http://doi.10.1007/s40615-020-00922-4.

Bryant, Susan L. 2019. "The Beauty Ideal: The Effects of European Standards of Beauty on Black Women." *Columbia Social Work Review* 11 (1): 80-91. https://doi.org/10.7916/cswr.v11i1.1933.

Carey, Roderick L. 2019. "Am I Smart Enough? Will I Make Friends? And Can I Even Afford It? Exploring the College-Going Dilemmas of Black and Latino Adolescent Boys." *American Journal of Education* 125 (3): 381-415. https://doi.org/10.1086/702740.

Clark, Langston. 2020. "Toward a Critical Race Pedagogy of Physical Education." *Physical Education and Sport Pedagogy* 25 (4): 439-450. https://doi.org/10.1080/1740 8989.2020.1720633.

Clark, Langston D., Martin P. Smith, and Louis Harrison, Jr. 2014. "The Contradiction of the Black Body: A Progressive Solution to Health Disparities in the Black Community." *Race, Gender & Class* 21 (1-2): 82-98. www.jstor.org/stable/43496961.

Collaborative for Academic, Social, and Emotional Learning (CASEL). 2021. "SEL: What Are the Core Competence Areas and Where Are They Promoted?" https://casel.org/sel-framework/.

Culp, Brian. 2016. "Social Justice and the Future of Higher Education Kinesiology." *Quest* 68 (3): 271-283. https://doi.org/10.1080/00336297.2016.1180308.

Culp, Brian. 2020a. "Thirdspace Investigations: Geography, Dehumanization, and Seeking Spatial Justice in Kinesiology." *Quest* 72 (2): 153-166. https://doi.org/10.10 80/00336297.2020.1729824.

Culp, Brian. 2020b. "Physical Education and Anti-Blackness." *Journal of Physical Education, Recreation & Dance* 91 (9): 3-5. https://doi.org/10.1080/07303084.2020.1811618.

Dei, George J. Sefa. 2017. *Reframing Blackness and Black Solidarities Through Anti-Colonial and Decolonial Prisms*. Cham, Switzerland: Springer.

Delpit, Lisa D. 2012. *"Multiplication Is for White People": Raising Expectations for Other People's Children*. New York: The New Press.

Dillard, Coshandra. 2020. "The Weaponization of Whiteness in Schools." *Learning For Justice* 65 (Fall 2020). www.learningforjustice.org/magazine/fall-2020/the-weaponization-of-whiteness-in-schools.

Dillard, Cynthia B. 2011. "Learning to (Re)member the Things We've Learned to Forget." In *Qualitative Inquiry and Global Crises*, edited by Norman K. Denzin and Michael D. Giardina, 226-243. Left Coast Press.

Du Bois, W.E.B. 1920. *The Souls of Black Folk*. New York: Penguin.

Dumas, Michael J. 2014. "'Losing an Arm': Schooling as a Site of Black Suffering." *Race Ethnicity and Education* 17 (1): 1-29. https://doi.org/10.1080/13613324.2013.850412.

Dumas, Michael J. 2016. "Against the Dark: Antiblackness in Education Policy and Discourse." *Theory Into Practice* 55 (1): 11-19. https://doi.org/10.1080/00405841.2016.1116852.

Dyer, Richard. 1997. *White*. London: Routledge.

Fitzpatrick, Katie, and Lorri J. Santamaría. 2015. "Disrupting Racialization: Considering Critical Leadership in the Field of Physical Education." *Physical Education and Sport Pedagogy* 20 (5): 532-546. https://doi.org/10.1080/17408989.2014.990372.

Flory, Sara B., and Nate McCaughtry. 2011. "Culturally Relevant Physical Education in Urban Schools: Reflecting Cultural Knowledge." *Research Quarterly for Exercise and Sport* 82 (1): 49-60. https://doi.org/10.1080/02701367.2011.10599721.

Ford, Donna. 2020. "Social-Emotional Learning for Black Students Is Ineffective When It Is Culture-Blind." *Diverse Issues in Higher Education*. Accessed February 6, 2020. https://diverseeducation.com/article/166341/.

Freire, P. 1970. *Pedagogy of the Oppressed*. New York: Seabury Press.

Gallagher, Charles A. 2003. "Color-Blind Privilege: The Social and Political Functions of Erasing the Color Line in Post Race America." *Race, Gender, and Class* 10 (4): 22-37. www.jstor.org/stable/41675099.

Garner, S. 2007. *Whiteness: An Introduction*. Abingdon: Routledge.

Garmon, M. Arthur. 2005. "Six Key Factors for Changing Preservice Teachers' Attitudes/Beliefs About Diversity." *Educational Studies* 38 (3): 275-286. https://doi.org/10.1207/s15326993es3803_7.

Hausburg, Taylor. 2020. "School-Community Collaboration: An Approach for Integrating and Democratizing Knowledge." *Penn GSE Perspectives on Urban Education* 17: 1-5. https://files.eric.ed.gov/fulltext/EJ1251601.pdf.

Harrison, Anthony Kwame. 2013. "Black Skiing, Everyday Racism, and the Racial Spatiality of Whiteness." *Journal of Sport & Social Issues* 37 (4): 315-339. https://doi.org/10.1177/0193723513498607.

Harrison, Louis, and Don Belcher. 2006. "Race and Ethnicity in Physical Education." In *Handbook of Physical Education*, edited by David Kirk, Doune Macdonald, and Mary O'Sullivan, 740-751. London: Sage. https://doi.org/10.4135/9781848608009.n41.

Harrison, Louis, Jr., and Langston Clark. 2016. "Contemporary Issues of Social Justice: A Focus on Race and Physical Education in the United States." *Research Quarterly for Exercise and Sport* 87 (3): 230-241. https://doi.org/10.1080/02701367.2016.1199166.

Hodge, Samuel R. 2014. "Ideological Repositioning: Race, Social Justice, and Promise." *Quest* 66 (2): 169-180. https://doi.org/10.1080/00336297.2014.898545.

Howard, Tyrone C. 2010. *Why Race and Culture Matters in Schools: Closing the Achievement Gap in America's Classrooms*. New York: Teachers College Press.

Hyland, Nora E. 2005. "Being a Good Teacher of Black Students? White Teachers and Unintentional Racism." *Curriculum Inquiry* 35 (4): 429-459. https://doi.org/10.1111/j.1467-873X.2005.00336.x.

Ignatiev, Noel. 1995. *How the Irish Became White*. New York: Routledge.

Jagers, Robert J. 2016. "Framing Social and Emotional Learning Among African-American Youth: Toward an Integrity-Based Approach." *Human Development* 59 (1): 1-3. https://doi.org/10.1159/000447005.

King, LaGarrett J. 2014. "When Lions Write History: Black History Textbooks, African-American Educators, & the Alternative Black Culture in Social Studies Education 1890-1940." *Multicultural Education* 22 (1): 2-11. https://files.eric.ed.gov/fulltext/EJ1065311.pdf.

Kunjufu, Jawanza. 2012. *There Is Nothing Wrong With Black Students*. Chicago: African American Images.

Ladson-Billings, Gloria. 2000. "Fighting for Our Lives: Preparing Teachers to Teach African American Students." *Journal of Teacher Education* 51 (3): 206-214. https://doi.org/10.1177/0022487100051003008.

Ladson-Billings, Gloria, and William F. Tate. 1995. "Toward a Critical Race Theory of Education." *Teachers College Record* 97 (1): 47-68. https://eric.ed.gov/?id=EJ519126.

Landi, Dillon, Shrehan Lynch, and Jennifer Walton-Fisette. 2020. "The A-Z of Social Justice Physical Education: Part 2." *Journal of Physical Education, Recreation & Dance* 91 (5): 20-27. https://doi.org/10.1080/07303084.2020.1739433.

Lynch, Shrehan, Sue Sutherland, and Jennifer Walton-Fisette. 2020. "The A-Z of Social Justice Physical Education: Part 1." *Journal of Physical Education, Recreation & Dance* 91 (4): 8-13. https://doi.org/10.1080/07303084.2020.1724500.

Matias, Cheryl E., and Daniel D. Liou. 2015. "Tending to the Heart of Communities of Color: Towards Critical Race Teacher Activism." *Urban Education* 50 (5): 601-625. https://doi.org/10.1177/0042085913519338.

Milner, H. Richard. 2016. "A Black Male Teacher's Culturally Responsive Practices." *The Journal of Negro Education* 85 (4): 417-432. https://doi.org/10.7709/jnegroeducation.85.4.0417.

Painter, Nell Irvin. 2010. *The History of White People.* New York: W.W. Norton.

Purdie-Vaughns, Valerie, and Gregory M. Walton. 2011. "Is Multiculturalism Bad for African Americans? Redefining Inclusion Through the Lens of Identity Safety." In *Moving Beyond Prejudice Reduction: Pathways to Positive Intergroup Relations,* edited by L.R. Tropp and R.K. Mallett, 159-177. American Psychological Association. https://doi.org/10.1037/12319-008.

Randall, Lynn, and Daniel B. Robinson. 2016. "An Introduction." In *Social Justice in Physical Education: Critical Reflections and Pedagogies for Change,* edited by Daniel B. Robinson and Lynn Randall, 1-14. Toronto: Canadian Scholars Press.

Roediger, David R. 2002. *Colored White: Transcending the Racial Past.* Berkeley: University of California Press.

Ross, K.M. 2020. "Call It What It Is: Anti-Blackness." *New York Times,* June 4, 2020. www.nytimes.com/2020/06/04/opinion/george-floyd-anti-blackness.html.

Reyes, Amanda. 2019. "Eugenic Visuality: Racist Epistemologies From Galton to 'The Bell Curve.'" *Amerikastudien/American Studies* 64 (2): 215-240. https://doi.org/10.33675/AMST/2019/2/6.

Sharpe, Christina. 2016. *In the Wake: On Blackness and Being.* Duke University Press.

Simmons, Dena. 2019. "Why We Can't Afford Whitewashed Social and Emotional Learning." *Education Update* 61 (4): 2-3. www.ascd.org/publications/newsletters/education_update/apr19/vol61/num04/Why_We_Can't_Afford_Whitewashed_Social-Emotional_Learning.aspx.

Singleton, Glenn E. 2013. *More Courageous Conversations About Race.* Thousand Oaks, CA: Corwin Press.

Sleeter, Christine. 2008. "An Invitation to Support Diverse Students Through Teacher Education." *Journal of Teacher Education* 59 (3): 212-219. https://doi.org/10.1177/0022487108317019.

Swartz, Ellen. 2009. "Diversity: Gatekeeping Knowledge and Maintaining Inequalities." *Review of Educational Research* 79 (2): 1044-1083. https://doi.org/10.3102/0034654309332560.

Spring, Joel. 2016. *Deculturalization and the Struggle for Equality.* 8th ed. Boston: McGraw-Hill.

Tatum, Beverly Daniel. 1997. *Why Are All the Black Kids Sitting Together in the Cafeteria? And Other Conversations About Race.* New York: Basic Books.

Tomlinson, Carol Ann. 2002. "Proficiency Is Not Enough: Balancing Excellence and Equity in No Child Left Behind." *Education Week* 22 (10): 36-37. www.edweek.org/leadership/opinion-proficiency-is-not-enough/2002/11.

Walton-Fisette, Jennifer L., Sue Sutherland, and Joanne Hill. 2019. *Teaching About Social Justice Issues in Physical Education.* Charlotte, NC: Information Age.

Warren, Chezare A., and Justin A. Coles. 2020. "Trading Spaces: Antiblackness and Reflections on Black Education Futures." *Equity & Excellence in Education* 53 (3): 382-398. https://doi.org/10.1080/10665684.2020.1764882.

Yancy, George. 2016. *Black Bodies, White Gazes: The Continuing Significance of Race in America*. 2nd ed. Lanham, MD: Rowman & Littlefield.

# Acknowledgments

We salute the Black pioneers in [physical] education who have created a path of excellence for us to write *Critical Race Studies in Physical Education*. We could not have completed this book without the courageous authors who contributed to this project. We genuinely appreciate your collective commitment to "level the playing field" for Black people to ensure we are seen as equals—thank you! We also want to thank Scott Wikgren and Skip Maier of Human Kinetics, and Thomas Lawson of SHAPE America for embracing our idea and showing authentic allyship when others lacked the courage to do so. Your support leaves us with hope for racial equality and social justice. Special thanks to Richard Allen for the expeditious formatting and proofreading of the book—indeed a time and lifesaver. Dr. Jenée Marquis, thank you for reformatting and implementing our Racial Equity Standards in your courses to help preservice teachers become culturally aware and able to meet the diverse needs of Black youth.

—Tara and Brian

I am grateful that my parents, Randolph and Priscilla Phifer, provided multiple opportunities to engage in quality education and physical activity programs, instilled Black girl pride, and demonstrated how to advocate for equal rights—thank you! To my favorite brother, Drake Phifer, thank you for always cheering for me no matter the magnitude of the endeavor.

Ronald Kinunen (Mr. K) and Dawn Indish, your quality physical education and sports programming made quite an impression.

To my dynamic duo, Akinyemi Blackshear and Afi Blackshear, I have always been proud to call you my sons. Thank you for allowing me to blend family into my work and joining me on the journey.

Causing "good trouble" with my collaborator, colleague, and friend, Dr. Brian Culp, thank you for cosigning as a soldier for social justice in spaces many dare not go. Please know that our work is changing the landscape of education. I look forward to the next project.

My significant other, Markus Green, is deserving of an award for enduring my endless chatter about this book. Thank you for your love, support, and understanding.

—Tara

"Not everything that is faced can be changed, but nothing can be changed until it is faced."

*James Baldwin*

Thank you to my parents, Randy and Patricia Culp, who saw the value in my work well before the most recent interest in justice-related issues. I would not be involved in this project without the great Dr. Tara Blackshear, who is the friend and colleague everyone needs. I acknowledge the dynamic contributors to this book who took the time to provide their perspectives while speaking truth to power. They follow in the footsteps of a host of Black scholars who have demonstrated courage in a discipline that still has significant work to do uncovering the experiences, aspirations, dreams, and motivations of Black youth.

—Brian

# Introduction

Extensive literature searches on Black youth in physical education result in zero texts. In other words, Black youth are not meaningfully represented in health and physical education. Black children are narrowly limited to two extremes, fostering polarized stereotypical narratives of athletically gifted or fat and inactive. As Black scholars, we are committed to equity, social justice, and anti-racist education with intentions to foster cultural awareness and competencies among physical education (PE) faculty and teacher candidates. The intentional focus on culturally relevant topics must occur to aid in moving transformative racial justice in education forward. Our in-boxes are flooded with requests to provide resources toward the betterment of Black lives in physical education. Hence, it is our duty to answer these calls for equity and social justice. *Critical Race Studies in Physical Education* centers Black youth and the complexities of Black culture into the conversation.

Amid the continued dehumanization of Blackness in American communities, Black Lives Matter and related movements have incited a renewed focus on the inequities and social injustices Black people encounter in all facets of society. Schools are no exception, because these sites are places where youth spend a large amount of time navigating attitudes, curriculum requirements, extracurricular activities, and social interactions. While the national and international dialogue for Black lives has gained traction, the attention to Black lives in physical education is still perilously and noticeably silent. Consequently, we created this text to elevate Black youth and to normalize positive experiences for Black students in physical education. This text has three aims:

1. To amplify critical issues that negatively affect Black people
2. To address the litany of intentional and covert racist practices directed toward Black youth
3. To provide culturally aware teaching strategies that affirm the worth of Black students

The primary audience for this book is preservice teachers and their instructors in physical education teacher education (PETE) programs who do not yet know how to accomplish the task of teaching for the success of Black students. Preservice teachers must be trained to identify and support pupils' diverse learning needs. This helps teachers identify and address barriers to learning and encourages linkages between the home and the school. Student teachers in university programs need information that will help them reflect and challenge biases as they explore notions of diversity, human dignity, social justice, and democratic citizenship for Black youth. PETE instructors need content that will help future teachers make connections while challenging misconceptions on teaching Black youth. Additionally, we feel that these teachers need to consider their actions in challenging situations and reflect on how they can begin their journey to become allies who take an active role in sustaining Black youths' lives.

Complementing Blackshear and Culp's (2021) transformative PETE standards developed to advance racial equity and social justice in physical education, eight case studies are presented to help reshape PETE programming with immediate implementation opportunities. Each case study includes background or contextual factors that help the reader understand the main characters and the presenting racial problem or problems. All the case studies are inspired by real events, but we changed the names of the people involved. We hope this will better allow the studies to serve as examples to prepare teachers to deal with similar situations in their own careers, rather than focus on specific individuals from the past. Although there is a dominant issue, several elements underpin each case study; they are designed to encourage robust dialogue among students and faculty and highlight the complexities of Black people's educational experiences. Each case study addresses the effects of anti-Black institutional policies and legislation (e.g., slavery, Jim Crow) related to schooling that have undermined the liberation of Black youth. A preview of each case study follows.

Training camps of racism and anti-racism run parallel and start early for both whites and Blacks. Blackshear's **case study 1, The "N-Word,"** confronts the weaponization of the term "nigger," used to terrorize and put Black people "in their place." Although this study focuses on the authentic experiences of a Black female physical educator, historical references, along with racist and anti-racist pedagogical experiences and practices, are embedded for preservice physical education teachers and PETE faculty to work toward racial justice. Perspectives of Black life are centered, including challenges, resilience, and contributions to education and American society—a stark contrast to the dearth of attention given to Black people in PETE programs. A prelude to the case studies that follow, case study 1 delivers subtleties of inequities aimed to foster critical analysis of the American educational system and its impact on Black children, while building up to a provocative climax sure to evoke a healthy range of emotions and dialogue.

Culp's captivating approach stokes the fires of injustice to magnify Black boys' soul-crushing experiences in **case study 2, Rational Fears or Provocative Tears?**—a poignant display of combative conditions Black children encounter in physical education environments. A female physical education teacher's alternate instruction plans stifle physical and intellectual growth of students who are otherwise vibrant, capable, and eager to learn. While supervising a student teacher, the lead teacher reproduces instigative and interrogating practices that foster student disengagement. Patterns of life-altering (and perhaps life-ending) events transpire, and blame pointed at normal middle school–aged children threatens the student teacher's inspiring ability to engage in culturally responsive practices. The stunning conclusion leaves an indelible impression on the consciousness of anyone committed to anti-racist pedagogies in physical education and beyond.

The narratives of Black competitive swimmers are often overlooked in the field of physical education. Highlighted in **case study 3, Gendered Racism, Racial Disparities, and the Black Body,** is an authentic example of Black girls' experiences when participating in sports and spaces perceived to be white. While dispelling myths that Black people do not swim, Quash presents a powerful illustration of the traumatic effects of gendered racism and the beginning stages of silencing Black girls. The suppression of Black girl voices erodes self-esteem and physical activity engagement and can continue over a lifespan. This leaves Black girls vulnerable and unprotected as they become Black womxn in society. Black girl trauma is regularly dismissed, changing trajectories from success-bound to precarious paths. A Black mother speaks up, understanding that if she does not, no one will—an unfortunate but recognized shared experience.

Elevating "Black is beautiful" ideals, Blackshear's **case study 4, Colorism and Protecting the CROWN,** confronts hegemonic forces of whiteness that marginalize Black beauty and negate physical activity engagement and well-being. Stratifications and subjugations of Black hair and skin hue further confine Black girls to socially constructed and culturally propagated fears of one's Blackness—apparent in this case study. Persistent efforts and pitfalls to protect the CROWN (Creating a Respectful and Open World for Natural Hair) and teacher engagement in culturally sustaining pedagogies are acknowledged to magnify the complexities when teaching Black girls in physical education. Sadness and misunderstandings transition to hope and change, as parallel journeys of self-love and allyship intersect to dismantle anti-Black thought, beliefs, and practice.

In **case study 5, "Nigga Under the Microscope": Crucial Conflict or Context-Specific?**, Angela K. Beale-Tawfeeq and Yvette Onofre broach the taboo subject on acceptability politics of Black and non-Black folks transforming racial slurs into terms of endearment, magnified in hip-hop music. Tackling the intersections of Teaching Personal and Social Responsibility (TPSR), allyship, and the complexities and metamorphosis of the term "nigger" in the PE setting, the case looks at the ramifications that "nigga" has on Black joy. A Latina PE teacher's savior complex creates a delusion of Black privilege, leading her to embrace all of Black culture without a deeper understanding of the cross-cultural power and etiology of words. This case study raises questions regarding efforts to "save" Black children and the discomforts caused by cultural appropriation.

Normalizing Black brilliance while challenging stereotypes of athletic superiority, intellectual inferiority, and maladaptive behaviors are presented in **case study 6, Black, Male, Queer, Athletic, and Academically Gifted**. Tara B. Blackshear, Afi C. Blackshear, and Akinyemi K. Blackshear introduce the challenges that Black males encounter in schools and in physical activity settings—challenges that are exacerbated when gay. This case study, defying toxic masculinities rooted in white heteronormativities, illustrates the positive impact that nurturing, inclusivity, and support have in fostering pathways to excellence and well-adjusted, confident Black boys of all sexual orientations. Escaping the limited portrayals of Black manhood takes a vigilant collective approach to transform deficit thinking and narratives promoted by hyperinsecurities of individuals who perform inclusivity but refuse to acknowledge and understand the diversity within Black groups.

Quash takes a delicate approach to highlight the challenges and detrimental experiences that Black transgender girls encounter in physical education in **case study 7, More Than a Bathroom: Black Transgender Student**. Sexist and anti-Black beliefs within the Black community, sometimes reinforced through Christian doctrine, push transgender girls and womxn to the farthest of margins among the marginalized. This case study, about a family facing a disproportionate amount of hate, violence, and ostracism because of difference and misunderstanding, calls for acceptance of fellow humans despite varying fundamental beliefs, and it serves as a reminder to physical educators that the gymnasium and activity spaces should be judgment-free and safe for all students.

Despite exaggerated claims that teacher education programs prepare teacher candidates to teach diverse learners, Grant's **case study 8, PETE Candidates Are Ill-Equipped to Teach Students in Black Urban Environments,** exposes the reality that student teachers lack preparation to teach Black students, causing them to grapple with accepting guaranteed teaching positions in predominantly Black schools. While some teacher candidates are culturally aware and have a strong desire to work with Black children, others would rather not. Can culturally responsive standards, approaches, and behaviors be achieved in PETE programs?

kali9/iStock/Getty Images

# CASE STUDY
# 1

# The "N-Word"

*Tara B. Blackshear*

Assata Jackson is a 28-year-old Black woman from Detroit living her dream of working with Black youth in schools. Growing up in an urban environment, she was familiar with the separate and unequal approaches to public school education, especially for Black children. Her parents removed her from public schools at the end of first grade after advice from Mrs. Scott, a Black teacher who had taught her older brother, Malcolm, to consider one of the area's private or parochial schools. Mrs. Scott's children attended parochial schools. She felt that the public school options were terrible, with ineffective teachers who had no interest in educating Black students. The climate was threatening; police presence and metal detectors were located at every entry point in the middle and high schools, sending a punitive rather than an academic message.

Knowledge of Mrs. Scott and other Black teachers' children not attending public schools profoundly affected Assata. Named after Assata Shakur, Assata's parents intentionally raised her to be independent, proud of her Blackness, and radically inquisitive. Her father would remind her, "We are raising you to be a strong independent woman, and as such, you should not play second fiddle to anyone." The family regularly discussed the complexities of race, particularly socially constructed concepts that position white people as better than others based on skin color and notions of hierarchy. Assata's father was clear in his messages regarding these beliefs: "A lot of white people want you to believe that you are less than. You're not." Hearing equity and social justice messages in her formative years and validation from her parents and community prepared Assata to become a formidable force when confronted with sexism and racism.

After graduating from high school, Assata attended Florida A&M University (FAMU) in Tallahassee. Malcolm was already in Atlanta attending Morehouse College, so they were not too far apart from each other. The choices to attend Historically Black Colleges and Universities (HBCUs) were also intentional efforts encouraged by Assata's parents to ensure a quality education that promoted Blackness and Black excellence with Black faculty.

Assata was undecided on a major when she arrived at FAMU. She initially thought she wanted to be a psychologist, but the amount of schooling and the thought of listening intently to people's issues all day did not excite her. After reflecting on the things she enjoyed, physical activity and sport were at the top of her list. Assata had participated in sports since age six, was on three varsity teams in high school, excelled in physical education (PE), and truly enjoyed physical activity and exercise. A visit to the department of health, physical education, recreation, and dance, where she met several Black women faculty members, including the department chair, solidified Assata's choice to major in health and physical education. Although Assata had attended predominantly Black schools in Detroit, her teachers were mostly white. Assata was overjoyed to see Black women with PhDs dominate a historically white and male field. These Black women professors had longevity at FAMU and were committed to Black excellence. They also encouraged Assata to earn her master's degree in physical education to increase her income opportunities, which she did at FAMU's expense. Assata had her firstborn two weeks before her master's commencement ceremony.

Married with a child, Assata and her husband, Magic, headed to Atlanta (a.k.a. the Black mecca), where Assata began her health and physical education teaching career at Ronald E. McNair High School. Assata had been encouraged to teach at a racially diverse and economically comfortable middle school in the district. Steve Jacobs, a white male PE director, tried to steer her toward these schools that he thought were less stressful for a first-year teacher. "You should consider Robert E. Lee or Confederate Middle, because there won't be as many discipline problems at those schools." Not convinced, and committed to teaching at a predominantly Black school in an urban environment, the other schools could not compete, especially after Assata met and connected with the Black woman principal, Dr. Gloria Hunter.

Assata had attended private schools with a uniform or strict dress code (e.g., socks or pantyhose and no jeans, gym shoes, or T-shirts), and she had not considered that students at McNair would wear what they wanted. The educational environment felt chaotic, with McNair ten times larger than

Assata's high school and seven times larger than the school where she conducted her student teaching. She was nervous as students had adult-sized bodies. To make matters worse, Assata looked very young. Dr. Hunter would often say, "I thought you were one of the kids."

The motto among faculty, "If you can teach at McNair, you can teacher anywhere."

Given her youth, size, and inexperience, Assata took a military-style approach, which was effective. After three months, Assata found her groove and started to bond with students. They could see that she cared about their well-being. She knew she was fulfilling her purpose. Once she lightened up after establishing routines, expectations, and built rapport, she and her students laughed about her previously strict methods. "Mrs. Jackson, remember how hard you came in here the first few weeks of school?" asked Chauncey, a six-foot-three male student athlete.

"I had to," said Assata, "I was looking up at six-feet tall students." Some of Assata's students were 20 years old and had been retained for various reasons—and she was only 24 at the time. Most teachers at the school, especially in physical education, had given up on them. Coach Pristell and Coach Williams, the two Black male gym teachers who rolled out the basketball every day, were more concerned about their athletes than teaching physical education.

The students knew Assata was different. At one point, Shaheed, a senior in Assata's team sports class, said she was the only PE teacher to take students outside and expose them to sports other than basketball. One day, out of the blue, he asked, "Why do you care?"

Assata replied, "You will appreciate it when you get older." During her tenure at McNair, Assata was instrumental in implementing an official PE dress code, adding to the curriculum, and including authentic assessments. Although the two white female PE teachers hired alongside Assata helped with dress code changes, they were not as invested in the students' success.

The expectation that high school physical education teachers must coach is universal. Once Assata had two kids, she transferred to a middle school, where there were no coaching expectations. Assata arrived at Bazoline E. Usher Middle School. The school, led by a Black woman principal, Dr. Jackie Wilkins, resonated with Assata, whose previous principal was also a Black woman. In contrast to McNair, however, most of the teachers and all the physical education teachers at Usher were Black, which she was excited to be part of. Despite teachers' hard work to uplift and educate students, many from challenging environments, the symptoms of low expectations in physical education plagued the school.

After four years in Atlanta, Assata relocates with her family to Lexington, Kentucky. She had left a big city where teaching jobs were plentiful, and now she finds herself taking the only physical education teaching position available in the county, at Booker T. Washington Elementary Magnet School. Assata is less than enthusiastic, given her undergraduate training in sixth through twelfth grade health and physical education and her passion for secondary school. However, she feels destined to work at a school named after another Black man and led by a Black woman principal, Annie Johnson. Assata's candidness about her dedication to Black children during the interview impressed Mrs. Johnson, such that she chased after Assata to offer her the job on the spot.

"Elementary is the toughest," says Mike Kingsley, the county public schools' physical education director, as he hands over a stack of elementary physical education resources to Assata. Like Assata, Mike gravitates toward secondary schools, and she understands his sentiments, although she knows she could teach anywhere given her experiences at McNair.

Unlike Assata's previous schools, and to her surprise, the school is racially, ethnically, and socioeconomically diverse, yet most students come from poor or working-class families. Many are Black or Hispanic, but the magnet school status attracts some affluent white families. The school is situated in a predominantly Black neighborhood, but a community of trailer park homes behind the school mostly consists of white families. White teachers refer to these students as "poor white trash" or "trailer park trash."

Extremely rowdy, Assata's third-grade class lines up to wait for their teacher, Ms. Simmons. Ms. Simmons, who is always late, did not value physical education. Assata tells students, "I need you to get in line and lower your voices." Billy, one of the kids from the trailer park, mumbles under his breath, "You don't tell me what to do, nigger." Shocked but calm, Assata replies like she would with her young children, spacing out the words "What. Did. You. Say?" Billy sheepishly hides behind a classmate but keeps watching her. Assata looks Billy in the eye and says emphatically, "I am not your nigger."

Billy loves physical education, like most of the other students, which Assata finds refreshing, given the energy level that she had to engage in to motivate students in secondary school. Billy's receptiveness to Assata and his enjoyment of class activities makes this interaction more upsetting. She thinks to herself "this child is a racist in training."

Realizing she has a teachable moment for Billy and an opportunity to protect Black students from this violent act, Assata knows the other students have their eyes focused on her. Assata continues, "I am not a nigger. *Nigger* is a very offensive racial slur used to try to hurt and dehumanize Black people. It is a legacy of slavery and an example of racism. This word is not acceptable and reflects poorly on those that choose to use this hateful term."

While some students giggle and others appear stunned, the Black students stand proudly that someone *finally* has come to their defense. Given the responses, Assata wonders how often Black students are called "nigger," by Billy or anyone else. She asks the students, "Why is it funny when I use the N-word but not when used by a classmate?"

This incident triggers the memory of an event that Assata experienced. It was the first time she was called a "nigger," at 19, while visiting Malcolm in Atlanta with three of her female friends from FAMU. They were minding their business, having a great time out on the town. Four white males in a car sped around a corner, nearly hitting them, yelling at the top of their lungs, "*NIGGERS!*" With a clear understanding of the historical significance and the hate behind this word, Assata had felt a sense of rage.

Assata hoped that Billy would not grow up and continue to inflict terror on Black people the way he did as an eight-year-old child in a physical education class. Later that evening, Assata calls Billy's parents to inform them of the racially charged language he directed toward her.

## Critical Race Study Discourse

1. Why do you think students giggled when Assata, and not Billy, said the N-word? How do you expect students to respond to Assata's question regarding the N-word? How do you think the phone call went with Billy's parents? Role-play the conversation between Assata and Billy's parents. Should there be any consequences for Billy? Why or why not? If yes, what should they be?

2. How should Assata handle the situation? Apply anti-racist pedagogy to address the critical issue(s). Identify the covert and overt examples of racism illustrated in the case study. What do you think the impact of being called a "nigger" had on Assata? Research responses that are triggered when a person is called a "nigger." Imagine if Assata were white? What do you think would be the response?

3. From where did the word *nigger* originate? Discuss the first time you used, were called, or heard the word *nigger*. How and why was it used?

4. Can you think of other marginalized groups that use a derogatory term as a term of endearment? Who? Are there parallels to the terms they used and the N-word?

5. What do you think would be the appropriate response for a Black person who has the N-word directed toward him or her?

6. Mark Twain is considered one of the great writers of American literature, and his book *The Adventures of Huckleberry Finn* is often cited as one of the great American novels. His book is also criticized and banned in some schools because of its use of racial stereotypes and the frequent use of the racial slur nigger. Reflect on whether you think these criticism are valid. Why or why not? What current television shows, videos, movies, and literature use the Black experience in a demeaning way for entertainment value.

7. Discuss the following quote by the 36th U.S. president, Lyndon B. Johnson: "If you can convince the lowest white man he is better than the best colored man, he won't notice you're picking his pocket. Hell, give him somebody to look down on, and he'll empty his pockets for you."

8. Conduct research and present a two- to five-minute elevator speech on the contributions of Assata Shakur, Booker T. Washington, Malcolm X, James Baldwin, Dr. Ronald E. McNair, Bazoline E. Usher, and HBCUs to Black excellence, liberation, and freedom.

9. Research the impact of gendered and racial representation in professional and academic spaces. Research Black women pioneers in physical education.

## References and Suggested Resources

Baldwin, James. 2017. *I Am Not Your Negro*. Raoul Peck, dir. Velvet Film.

Bottoms, Greg. 2019. *Lowest White Boy*. Morgantown: West Virginia University Press.

Clark, Langston, Marcus W. Johnson, Latrice Sales, and LaGarrett King. 2020. Remember the Titans: The Lived Curriculum of Black Physical Education Teacher Education Scholars in the U.S. *Sport, Education and Society* 25 (5): 501-517. https://doi.org/10.1080/13573322.2019.1617126.

Kennedy, Randall. 2003. *Nigger: The Strange Career of a Troublesome Word*. New York: Vintage Books.

Lewis, Donna Williams. 1985. "Centenarian Bazoline Usher Recalls Her Days as an Educator." *Atlanta Constitution*. December 26, 1985.

*Niggers in the White House*. 1903. [author unknown]. https://en.wikipedia.org/wiki/Niggers_in_the_White_House#/media/File:Kentucky_New_Era_3_13_03.png

"Ronald McNair." Biography. Last modified September 14, 2020. www.biography.com/astronaut/ronald-mcnair.

Shakur, Assata. 2014. *Assata: An Autobiography*. London: Zed Books.

Smock, Raymond W. 2009. *Booker T. Washington: Black Leadership in the Age of Jim Crow*. Chicago: Ivan R. Dee.

Tyree, Tia C.M., and Christopher D. Cathcart, eds. 2014. *HBCU Experience—The Book: A Collection of Essays Celebrating the Black College Experience.* Xlibris Corp.

X, Malcolm, M.S. Handler, Alex Haley, and O. Davis. 1992. *The Autobiography of Malcolm X* (First Ballantine Books trade edition). New York and Toronto: Ballantine Books.

© Shutterstock

# Rational Fears or Provocative Tears?

*Brian Culp*

A common sight in the Henderson Middle School gymnasium was the weekly planning period meltdown by the head physical education teacher, Amber Rossdale. Walking to her office, she pronounced to no one in particular: "I swear that third period and fourth period is going to be the death of me," "They're just rude, especially the boys," or "I wish the administration would crack down because I refuse to do it anymore." Student teacher Christina followed Ms. Rossdale pensively, fully knowing what was going to come next: 30 minutes of lament, 29 minutes of blame, and 1 minute of dubious advice. The commentary each week was the same: "The only thing good about this transfer has been the money," "No offense to you, 'cause I know you're from here, but I don't know what people are teaching these kids at home," "You're a smart girl—a good girl, exactly like I was when I got started," "You've got a future," and "Don't waste your time in a working situation like this."

Three months into student teaching, Christina was feeling conflicted about her placement and her supervisor. After being accepted into the physical education teacher education (PETE) program a year ago, she went against the advice of her cohort and requested to teach in the Henderson community. The university practicum coordinator even had reservations. Up until a week before her placement, Christina was asked if she was sure she wanted to be at Henderson and was reminded that it wasn't too late to change to another site.

Christina was undaunted. She grew up in Henderson. Despite the depictions of Henderson, a predominantly Black community with its schools being stereotyped as "inner-city," "rough," "ghetto," and "thugged-out," Christina saw positives about Henderson that outsiders often missed. While Henderson did not have many resources, the community was proud of its history as a center of Black culture. Decades earlier, prominent Black businesses, churches, newspapers, and theaters positioned Henderson as a regional center of commerce and entrepreneurship. Despite this well-known history, Ms. Rossdale, a former teacher of the year who was white, like Christina, held a toxic bias against the students in the school. While Christina ignored her actions for the sake of keeping the peace, she felt that Ms. Rossdale was more invested in being a tragic figure than meeting the needs of students.

The two were now sitting quietly across from one another in the office. Christina looked past Ms. Rossdale to the empty gym, where a clock hung protected by a wire guard. Below the clock was a sign in bold letters: **The clock is working. Are you?** The juxtaposition was not lost on Christina. In a few minutes, students would be entering the gym looking to break away from their prescriptive lessons, but the gym would resemble more of a work camp.

Ms. Rossdale was preparing for conflict. "So you know Christina, fourth period is going to test us like they always do. Make sure that B plan is ready for Rashad, Bennie, and Alfonso. You're going to need to separate them after roll and before they group up. In fact, because the school is a few days late with testing, we might want to think about that for all of them today because they won't be focused."

"B plan." Christina knew what it was. In other words, a conscious focus on discipline and watching students. Lessons were to be simple and non-challenging for students. Whether students learned anything was optional. The goal was to make sure that the 40 students who came into the gym left at the end of the class with no issues. Christina didn't know why Ms. Rossdale called it "B plan." It was the same plan that took place in every class.

The bell rang. Students from the fourth period slowly entered the gym and began walking around for a warm-up. One voice always stood out from the rest.

"Ms. ROSS-DALE! I waved at you the other day in the parking lot. Why didn't you wave back?" Rashad is hard to ignore. He is taller and stockier than the other eighth-grade boys his age and wears to class a variety of retro T-shirts that he matches with a corresponding color wristband. Nearly every teacher in the school loves his positivity and eagerness to help, even though his coordination is noticeably behind his cognitive skill. Rashad is a talker—specifically about engineering. A few months ago, he won a local Lego building competition and now spends time after school being mentored by people who want to work with someone they consider a budding prodigy.

Rashad attempts to fist-bump Ms. Rossdale as he walks closer to her. She rebuffs him. Glaring at him as he passes in front of her, she asks, "First of all, what are you supposed to be doing, and why aren't you doing it?"

He quickly counters, "Don't worry, Ms. Rossdale, I'm going to do warm-up. How are you, Ms. Christina?" Rashad puts his fist out again, this time with Christina obliging the gesture.

Seeing the act, Ms. Rossdale again looks at Rashad disapprovingly and says sternly, "Her name is Ms. Morris, and you should be walking faster. In fact, ALL OF YOU SHOULD BE WALKING FASTER. Every day you folks show up in this class, it's like you got lead in your pants. Remember, you're walking on the INSIDE path of the stations." As Christina walks around with students to take roll, she hears them complain about Ms. Rossdale out of her earshot. The words from their frustrated mouths ring a familiar chorus:

"I know she's not talking about me."

"She's always looking at us like we're going to do something."

"I'm tired of coming to this stank gym with this lame stuff."

"When y'all going to play some music in here?"

A student speaks directly to Christina. "Ms. Morris, I want you to be our teacher. I'm tired of Ms. Rossdale."

After the warm-up is completed, students gather at the center of the circle and wait for directions. Under the watchful eye of Ms. Rossdale, Christina explains to students the station activities for the class period, which for this day is a mixture of fitness and hands-on activities. As she finishes, Christina begins the process of grouping students. Since they have already worked in assigned groups earlier in the unit, Christina thinks that giving students a choice on who to partner with would be a good way to end a long week. After motioning to the class to stand up, partner into threes, and choose a station, Rashad, Bennie, and Alfonso group up and begin moving before being stopped.

"Boys, you can't be together," Ms. Rossdale exclaims. She then points at Bennie and Alfonso. "Bennie, I want you to go work with Courtney and Tanisha over on the other side of the gym where I can see you. Alfonso, you can start over here next to me with Austin and Mike."

Bennie gives an inquisitive look to Ms. Rossdale and then shakes his head in bewilderment before remarking, "Ms. Rossdale, I already worked with Austin and Mike this week. Can't we just keep our group together? It's Friday."

Alfonso chimes in, "Yeah, Ms. Rossdale, can we just work together like we want today?"

Pausing to look at the boys for a brief second, Ms. Rossdale relents. "Okay, you can both go back to where you were. We have a couple people missing today, so you can work in a group of two. Rashad, though, will be working with Annalise and Ms. Morris."

Bennie laughs. "Ha, Rashad, you gotta work with Ms. Christina." He and Alfonso start off running to their station. Christina turns to Ms. Rossdale and asks why she is now instructing at one station instead of taking on the whole class. Ms. Rossdale explains, "Yeah, the original plan was for you to go around and give feedback to everyone, but some of these kids like to be shifty once they think they know what they're doing. It's probably good that you can stay with Rashad and Annalise. Rashad is beginning to act like a pit boss running this school, and Annalise told me before class that she's not feeling well, so whatever we get out of her today will be what it is." Ms. Rossdale starts walking away but turns back. "And whatever you do, be careful letting them touch you. These kids are walking petri dishes."

Midway into the class, Ms. Rossdale approaches Christina and tells her to take over for the rest of the period because she is going to the equipment room outside the gym to take inventory. As Ms. Rossdale leaves the gym, Christina thinks: "She forgot to ask about Rashad and Annalise." Annalise had said that she was going to sit down on the bleachers for a few minutes, which left Christina and Rashad together. Now that Christina is tasked with watching the whole class, Rashad is alone—which he quickly noticed. "Ms. Christina, I don't have a group. Can I go over to the golf station with Bennie and Alfonso?" Christina ponders Rashad's request and decides that there isn't much time left in class and that there's no need to bother Ms. Rossdale. Besides, a few minutes of Rashad working with his friends wouldn't be the worst thing in the world. She reminds him of the rules of the station—namely, remembering to putt from the designated line and making sure that one person in the group is always watching the door in case a putt goes out of the room.

In watching Rashad run off in excitement, Christina wonders for a moment if Rashad heard all her instructions clearly. She is worried that she and Ms. Rossdale made a hasty decision to put the golf station near the open main doors. Normally, the doors aren't open, but May is abnormally warm this year, necessitating added ventilation in the gym. Rashad arrives at the golf station and lets Bennie and Alfonso know that he is in the group.

After each of them takes a few turns at the designated line for the putt to the hole, the boys become bored and decide to challenge themselves. Bennie is first, setting up his putt nearly 20 yards behind the original designated line for the station. This makes the challenge of putting the ball into the hole significantly more difficult. However, none of the boys are worried about this; it is time to have some fun.

Bennie line up and putts. The ball rolls true and hits the back bumper, stopping an inch short of the hole. "Bow to a real pro!" Bennie says as he smiles at Alfonso and Rashad, before adding, "You ain't gonna be able to get inside that."

Rashad walks over to Bennie, motioning to him to hand over the putter and the extra ball he has in his pocket. Nodding at his friends, he lines up next to Bennie and places the ball down to prepare for the long putt. Rashad then lectures, "Y'all doing it the wrong way, I bet if you put your hands on the end of the club like they do on TV, when you hit it, it'll go farther. It's the laws of physics."

"It's the laws of crazy," Alfonzo replies. "It's a putt. You got the wrong club. Besides, your aim is off."

"Whatever, man, you're a hater," Rashad snipes back. Rashad draws the putter back and hits the ball with his head up and the face open. As he watches the ball jump from the floor and bounce through the doors into the hallway, Alfonzo and Bennie begin to laugh. Rashad starts to panic and runs toward the door muttering, "We need to go get that ball."

"We?" Alfonzo replies, grinning. "We didn't do anything. You hit the ball outside."

"But it's our station," Rashad shouts. "If we don't get this ball, Ms. Christina is going to see us, and we are all going to be in trouble." Rashad is now in the hallway waving his hand to Alfonzo and Bennie to meet him.

"He's got a point." Bennie starts running to meet Rashad. "You going to stay there, Alfonzo?"

Alfonzo has no desire to leave his spot. "Someone has to be around, or Ms. Christina will think something is up. I'll be here. Y'all have fun."

Bennie and Rashad are in the hallway facing a split corridor. Bennie points to the left. "I think it might be down there next to that trash can."

"Cool," Rashad answers. "I'll go the other way."

The boys go their separate directions. After walking the length of the corridor and finding nothing, Rashad starts walking back to the gym. He looks down the other corridor to see if Bennie had had better luck in his search. Bennie is walking back toward him, proudly cradling the golf ball in his outstretched hands. A figure becomes visible behind him. Unaware of this development, Bennie shouts to Rashad. "LOOK WHAT I FOUND!"

The figure speaks. "What did you find, Bennie? I think I found someone who is clearly not where they are supposed to be!" Ms. Rossdale's voice pierces the hallway as tension rises in the air. She continues, "Keep on walking to the gym Bennie; don't even turn your guilty face around. Not one word. You're going in the book!" The "book" is Ms. Rossdale's way of telling students that they will be written up and reported to the assistant principal for discipline issues. It means that a phone call will be made.

"What?" Bennie stammers in disbelief. "You gonna call my parents? For real? We were just looking for the ball. It got hit out of the gym. Nobody got hurt. I wasn't even the one that hit it!" Ms. Rossdale and Bennie are now facing Rashad, who is nodding in agreement with Bennie's assessment of the situation.

Rashad walks closer to the two and gently places his hand on Ms. Rossdale's arm to plead his case. "Ms. Rossdale, it was my fault. I was trying to hit the ball from further back, and it just went out of the gym."

Ms. Rossdale quickly jerks her arm away, repulsed. Her voice begins to escalate as she moves away from Rashad. "Do not EVER touch me, boy!" Bennie starts to move in between the two with his hands up.

As this is happening, Christina and Alfonzo are walking through the gym doors just in time to see Ms. Rossdale shoving Bennie away from her. She shouts loud enough for everyone in earshot to hear. "You see what they're doing! They're ganging up on me. I'm calling the resource officer. I knew I couldn't trust them to do the basics. All of you are getting kicked out of school!" Turning to Christina, she adds, "Don't let them out of your sight! You are going to need to talk to the resource officer and principal." Ms. Rossdale immediately begins running toward her office. Christina and the boys stand in the hallway, looking at one another.

Alfonzo shakes his head and remarks, "I wish Ms. Rossdale was *white like you*, Ms. Christina."

## Critical Race Study Discourse

1. How should Christina address this situation? What are the critical issues at play in this case study?

2. Negrophobia is fear and aversion to Black people and Black culture. The phobia is fed by the brute caricature that Black men are savage, violent predators who target helpless victims, in particular white women. (Visit the section on the brute caricature compiled at https://ferris.edu/jimcrow/brute/.) Would you consider the behaviors and actions of Ms. Rossdale characteristic of this phobia, or do you feel these behaviors and actions are indicative of something else? In what ways might negrophobic caricatures have informed Christina's approach with Rashad?

3. Reflecting on this case study and how it ended, how do you think you would respond to the resource officer and assistant principal?

4. Alfonzo, at the end of this case study, turned to Christina and remarked that he wished that Ms. Rossdale was a white person like Christina. What is your interpretation of Alfonzo's assessment? What implications do you think this statement has for the promotion of racial equity and justice in teaching physical education? Are there any negative consequences to Alfonzo's statement?

5. Conduct research on the concept of "Black joy." With a partner or a group, present to each other a two- to five-minute synopsis of what you found. Brainstorm strategies on how you would promote this concept for the benefit of your students in physical education.

6. What do you think the impact of Ms. Rossdale's actions will be on the students in this case study and Christina? Identify teaching behaviors, school policies, and physical education practices that contribute to the school-to-prison pipeline.

7. After reading this case study, what recommendations do you have for Ms. Rossdale? Christina? Rashad? Henderson Middle School?

## References and Suggested Resources

Blackshear, Tara B., and Brian Culp. 2021. "Transforming PETE's Initial Standards: Ensuring Social Justice for Black Students in Physical Education." *Quest* 73 (1): 22-44. https://doi.org/10.1080/00336297.2020.1838305.

Cooper, Brittney. 2020. *Eloquent Rage: A Black Feminist Discovers Her Superpower.* New York: Picador.

Fanon, Frantz. 2008. *Black Skin, White Masks.* New York: Grove Press.

Ferris State University. "Jim Crow Museum of Racist Memorabilia." www.ferris.edu/HTMLS/news/jimcrow/.

Painter, Nell Irvin. 2010. *The History of White People.* New York: W.W. Norton.

Smiley, CalvinJohn, and David Fakunle. 2016. "From "Brute" to "Thug": The Demonization and Criminalization of Unarmed Black Male Victims in America." *Journal of Human Behavior in the Social Environment* 26 (3-4): 350-366. https://doi.org/10.1080/10911359.2015.1129256.

Yancy, G. (2016). *Black Bodies, White Gazes: The Continuing Significance of Race in America.* 2nd ed. Lanham, MD: Rowman & Littlefield.

© Shutterstock

# 3

# Gendered Racism, Racial Disparities, and the Black Body

*Tiffany Monique Quash*

Ashley Mandela is a Black ninth-grade interscholastic swimmer attending Wildcat High School, where most students come from middle-class neighborhoods. The diversity within the high school is achieved by busing in students from primarily Black neighborhoods. Ironically, the area was historically for Black people. The homes were built on a landfill in the early 1970s. Gentrification, however, leaves the impression that the community has always been white. The closest high school to Ashley is 10 minutes away; however, Ashley and some of her peers are bused to school 30 minutes away.

The decisions made within the school district are often discussed in Ashley's household because of the historical connection her mother and many other Black families in her neighborhood have. Ashley's school is one of a few that still has swimming as part of the physical education (PE) curriculum, which has continued because two Black students drowned on a school field trip many years ago. Ashley's mother, Linda Mandela, was once a teacher within the district and regularly attends school district meetings. Ms. Mandela once taught at Wildcat High with many of the current teachers.

This case study consciously removes the "e" and replaces it with an "x" in womxn to focus on the experiences of womxn without being subjugated to the experiences of men.

Despite being a single-parent household, Ms. Mandela provides a strong Black womxn support system for Ashley, academically and athletically. They both wear their hair naturally; Ms. Mandela sports a small 'fro, and Ashley wears shoulder-length locks. Ms. Mandela and Ashley are aware of the assumptions people make about their family, specifically about being Black and having a single-parent household. On free weekends, Ms. Mandela and Ashley either visit a college or university campus, go hiking, or do something else outdoors.

Ashley and her mother are frequently asked questions about their hair by both Black and white people. The types of questions and how they are asked vary by race. From Black friends and family, questions focus on how to maintain Black hair given Ashley is in the pool for extended hours at a time. "How do you keep your hair from getting nappy?" asked her neighbor. "Girl, I don't have the face to wear my hair naturally," said her mother's friend. People who are white typically ask questions like "How do you wash your hair?" or "Can I touch your hair?" At times, they touch it or try to touch it without asking—something that should *never* be done to Black womxn and Black girls.

In addition to Ashley's hair, her choice to swim is often questioned, or people assume she is not a swimmer. Everyone thinks she is either a runner or plays basketball. When Ashley corrects people and insists that she is a swimmer, they sometimes squint their eyes and say, "I see it now! You have really broad shoulders!"

The comments people make about Ashley's body never bothered her until high school, but she has always understood the importance of swimming. When Ashley was six months old, Ms. Mandela made the conscious choice to acclimate Ashley to swimming pools, make her aware of water safety rules, and enroll her in learn-to-swim lessons. In the parent and child swim classes, Ms. Mandela would often be the only Black adult in the course. At times, swim instructors were overly concerned and cautious about Ms. Mandela and Ashley's participation. Ms. Mandela was not a strong swimmer, but she understood the value of water safety education and the racial disparities in drowning statistics. Ashley quickly gained confidence in the water and joined the local swim team at the age of five.

Being one of the few Black swimmers representing her local club team and high school team in the district and at state swim meets never surprises Ashley or Ms. Mandela. Ashley is both athletically and academically gifted; she has always remained academically eligible for attending swim meets. Although Ms. Mandela does not fully understand competitive swimming, she attends all practices and swim meets with her daughter. Ms. Mandela recognizes that other parents and guardians might perceive this as "hovering," but she knows what people are capable of when a parent is not around.

Randolph-Macon Woman's College Swim Team (Lynchburg, Virginia)

This swim team picture is from the author's personal collection. The experiences of being a Black womxn swimmer are often unrecognized by coaches and under researched by academics.

During swim meets, Ms. Mandela hears disparaging comments from white onlookers in the stands when Ashley competes. Comments she's heard include:

"That nigger isn't wearing the appropriate swim attire."

"That girl needs to be disqualified; you know Black people do not swim!"

"Didn't that pickaninny already win an event?"

"There that girl goes, again!"

"We can't have anything of our own. They always want to take what's ours."

Commenters don't seem to know that an all-Black swim team won the state championship in 1974, and recently, an all-Black swim team in neighboring Delaware was in contention for the title.

Instead of interjecting, Ms. Mandela remains silent and decides not to tell Ashley, the coaches, or swim officials about the comments she hears during the swim meets. Sometimes these remarks are so loud that officials and coaches can hear them. Rather than reprimanding or reminding the heckler about the code of conduct, coaches and officials look for a reaction on Ms. Mandela's face to determine if anything should be done. The coaches and officials' inability to redirect the white commenters irritates Ms. Mandela, but it is the responsibility of those in leadership to handle this misconduct and not hers.

Near the end of the season, Ashley asks her mother if she can attend practices alone, with Ms. Mandela arriving toward the end of practice to pick her up. Although the thought of not sitting through Ashley's practice is uncomfortable, Ms. Mandela knows that Ashley has to build her confidence. They agree that it is time for Ashley to begin holding her own on the deck as she prepares for collegiate swimming in the future.

The head team swim coach at Wildcat High is a white cisgender man, Paul Ross. He was a first-year teacher when Ms. Mandela taught at Wildcat High, but many years have passed, and now Paul is head of the PE department. They had a cordial working relationship during her tenure, but Ms. Mandela knows that the PE department has had challenges recruiting and retaining people of color to the faculty. Even though Ashley is on the swim team, she is scheduled to take ninth-grade PE with Paul during the school day.

A new face at the school, Janelle Pendergrass, is the first Black swim coach (head or assistant) for the district. Janelle, a former collegiate swimmer at a Division I institution, wears locks and has experience coaching high school and club teams. There are four PE teachers in the school, and Janelle is one of two female teachers but is the only Black PE teacher.

The responsibilities of PE teachers at Wildcat High include a full teaching load, one planning period, and coaching at least one team. Because of Janelle's experience, coaching swimming naturally fits into her repertoire.

During Janelle's first swim practice with Paul and the team, Paul formally introduces the team to Janelle. When Paul gets to Ashley, he says, "Ashley is our superstar, with interesting hair just like yours. I call her Buckwheat. Ya know, from the Little Rascals! Y'all know what I'm saying!" The team laughed, and Ashley chuckled uncomfortably. Paul had called Ashley "Buckwheat" during PE class, as well, and Ashley had the same reaction: a chuckle. As the new person on staff and to the team, Janelle wants to be viewed as a team player, so she smiles at Paul. Janelle notices how uncomfortable Ashley looks after Paul's comment.

During her PE class, Ashley frequently asks to go to the nurse because she is not feeling well. She returns just before the class ends. Each time this happens, Paul says to Ashley, "You have to show up to get your grade, Ashley." Ashley is uncomfortable with his remarks, but she is unsure how to approach the situation.

Back on the deck during introductions, the only other Black (but mixed-race) swimmer, Becky, continued with the anti-Black commentary. "You need to get some lotion for those ashy legs. Ashley is ashy." Peers began laughing and chanting, "Ashley is ashy, Ashley is ashy, Ashley is ashy." It takes everything Ashley can muster not to break down and cry.

As the season continues, Ashley's grades drop from straight A's to C's. Given the eligibility requirements, Janelle says, "Paul, I am really concerned about Ashley's academic eligibility. Do you know what is going on or how we can help her?"

Paul responds, "She's Black, comes from a single-parent family, and she's lower-income. She will get into a Division I school just fine because of her swim times." Janelle's face showed her shock at Paul's comment, and he immediately continued, "I mean . . . I'm not a racist. You know swimming is a numbers game based on one's speed. Buckwheat will be just fine." Appalled by Paul's response, Janelle wants to approach Ashley to check in with her, but she is unsure how to address the "Buckwheat" comments.

Being the new teacher and the only Black PE teacher, Janelle begins to pick up on how other PE teachers treat Black student athletes versus white student athletes. The basketball and football teams are majority Black boys. Academically, the majority of each team is academically ineligible, but the white coaches have figured out a system to get them through. The girls' basketball team is also majority Black, but they have to work harder than the boys—and they are given the boys' extra jerseys from the year before to wear as uniforms. The track and field team is majority Black boys and girls. Overall, there is an expectation that they will always win within the district because these teams are Black and they have the "muscles" to defeat other teams. However, the swim, lacrosse, field hockey, and wrestling teams are sports that Janelle's colleagues don't take seriously because the majority of the athletes are white. Internally, Janelle questions her colleagues' teaching philosophy and wonders how Paul could have climbed the ladder to being a department chair based on this belief system.

Janelle wants to reach out to Ashley and Ms. Mandela but is unsure of the correct protocol for doing so. Being a new PE teacher and assistant swim coach, Janelle feels conflicted and about bringing Paul's behaviors up to her principal, who is also a white cisgender man. She knows that if she takes this situation to the principal, she could be marked as the "angry black womxn" or appear to be unable to deal with team conflict. Janelle wants to be an advocate for Ashley, but how can she do so at the beginning of her career?

Ashley knows she is suffering academically and having a negative social experience on the swim team. Older swimmers and other Black students begin to chide her because of the increase of muscle mass she has gained due to the intensity of her training. People call her beefy and question her gender identity and sexuality. During swim meets, her team members and Paul "joke" with her and say, "Has anyone seen Ashley?" when she is clearly the only Black swimmer on the deck or is standing in front of the person speaking. Her experience is becoming more painful than enjoyable. She thinks that if she speaks up to either coach, she will be kicked off the team, or that everyone will think she is overly sensitive. Ashley knows that she has to tell her mother what's going on, but she thinks that if she holds out just a little bit longer that things will change.

Ashley begins to disengage with her teammates during practices and competitions so she can navigate throughout the season. Practices become a place that is mentally exhausting rather than physically exhausting. After a few weeks, Ashley cannot take the comments anymore. She speaks to her mother about the interactions with her swim team and her peers at school. Her mother asks if she has spoken to her coaches. Ashley responds, "How can I speak to Coach Ross when he calls me Buckwheat in front of the team?"

Ashley's mother is shocked and asks Ashley, "Are these comments made to you only by your coaches? Has anyone in your PE class or on the swim team made these comments to you?" Ashley nods yes, and she describes how her other teachers and peers treat her. Immediately, Ms. Mandela schedules a conference with teachers for the following week.

During the next school day, Janelle notices Ashley's behavior and asks Paul if he has seen anything different about Ashley. Paul responds, "Ashley is just plateauing in her training. I see it all the time, and this is nothing new for an athlete built like her. She will bounce back."

Unsatisfied with his response, Janelle asks, "Do you think she is upset about the name you called her a few weeks back?"

Paul stands up and says, "Buckwheat? She knew I was kidding with her. Listen, if you want to connect with the students, you have to give them little nicknames to make them feel good. I need to finish my lesson plan and write practice for today. Do you have anything else you need to talk to me about?" Seeing that Paul is irritated with her question, Janelle shakes her head and continues her lesson plan. This is the second time that a conversation between Janelle and Paul makes him appear physically uncomfortable.

The next week arrives, and it is time for the parent–teacher conference. All the teachers are white, except Janelle. When Ms. Mandela asks the teachers if they have noticed a behavioral change between Ashley and her peers, they say that they are not aware of any moments of conflict or confrontation. Each teacher (except Janelle) says that they have not noticed any changes in Ashley and that any changes are more than likely related to it being her first-year in high school—and probably hormones.

Unsatisfied with the response, Ms. Mandela asks the PE teachers if they have witnessed anything on the deck or heard anything in the locker room that would explain a change in Ashley's behavior. Paul responds, "Ms. Mandela, you remember how it was when you were a teacher here. High school kids are challenging. Ashley's training will get better, but it is normal for an athlete to plateau. Plus, she goes to the nurse during her PE class, where she gets docked points for her lack of participation. Ashley has put on some weight. Have you considered taking her to a nutritionist?" Shocked by the comments and suggestions, Ms. Mandela shakes her head no. Ms. Mandela turns to Janelle and asks her, "Have you noticed anything different about Ashley?"

Janelle knows exactly what prompted Ms. Mandela to ask this question, and she carefully chooses her words to express the reality of Ashley's experience from her perspective. Janelle says, "Ms. Mandela, being the only Black swimmer on the Wildcat High's swim team in the school's recent history, and even in the district, can be challenging. This includes understanding what it means to be a Black athlete, a Black girl, and an excellent Black swimmer. I wonder if there are words that Ashley has shared with you about her experience?" This is the best that Janelle can do while sitting in front of her colleagues to help prompt Ms. Mandela to share Ashley's experience. Ms. Mandela understands this coded language and responds, "Actually, there is a list of a few concerns that Ashley shared with me." Ms. Mandela pulls out a list that includes Paul's comments and reasons Ashley goes to see the nurse during her PE class.

## Critical Race Study Discourse

1. What elements of risk are involved by Janelle discussing what she has witnessed? How should Janelle address Ms. Mandela's question in the meeting with her colleagues?

2. What critical issues are at play in this case study regarding the experiences of Ashley Mandela, Linda Mandela, and Janelle Pendergrass? What steps could Janelle have taken before the meeting?

3. The exploitation of Black womxn's bodies predates the enslavement of African people and Black bodies. Identify the areas of this case study that address such examples. What biases have you heard when discussing the athletic capabilities of Black girls and womxn?

4. Discuss the intersections of race, gender, and swimming. What is the overall perception of Black womxn and girls participating in swimming?

5. Write, reflect, and discuss the behaviors of Paul. What would you do in Janelle's situation upon hearing Paul's comments?

6. Think about Buckwheat and identify similar Black television characters depicted in the 1930s and 1940s. Compare and contrast Black television characters of the past to Black characters today.

7. Identify and provide examples of the differences between systemic and systematic. How can systematic and systemic racism persist in physical education and physical education activities?

# References and Suggested Resources

Bullard, Robert D. 1994. "Essays on Environmental Justice: Environmental Racism and 'Invisible' Communities." *West Virginia Law Review* 96: 1037.

Dabiri, Emma. 2019. *Don't Touch My Hair.* Allen Lane.

Dawson, Kevin. 2018. *Undercurrents of Power: Aquatic Culture in the African Diaspora.* Philadelphia: University of Pennsylvania Press.

Dosekun, Simidele. 2021. "Beyond Black Beauty Politics: A Review of *Don't Touch My Hair* by Emma Dabiri." *Journal of African Cultural Studies* 33 (1): 109-110. https://doi.org/10.1080/13696815.2020.1727312.

Gilchrist, Julie, and Erin M. Parker. 2014. "Racial/Ethnic Disparities in Fatal Unintentional Drowning Among Persons Aged ≥29 years—United States, 1999-2010." *Morbidity and Mortality Weekly Report (MMWR)* 63 (19): 421-426. www.cdc.gov/mmwr/preview/mmwrhtml/mm6319a2.htm?s_cid=mm6319a2_w.

Goebel, Taylor. 2021. "Friends Boasts First All-Black Swimming Team to Make State Medal Podium." *Delware Live: Our State Our News Our Home,* March 15, 2021. https://delawarelive.com/2021/03/15/friends-boasts-first-all-black-swimmer-team-to-make-state-medal-podium/.

Lawrence, Suzanne Malia. 2005. "African American Athletes' Experiences of Race in Sport." *International Review for the Sociology of Sport* 40 (1): 99-110. https://doi.org/10.1177/1012690205052171.

Malina, R.M. 2009. "Children and Adolescents in the Sport Culture: The Overwhelming Majority to the Select Few." *Journal of Exercise Science & Fitness* 7 (2): S1-S10. https://doi.org/10.1016/S1728-869X(09)60017-4.

Norwood, Dawn M. 2010. "I Am Not My Hair . . . Or Am I?: Exploring the Minority Swimming Gap." PhD diss., University of Tennessee Knoxville, 2010. https://trace.tennessee.edu/utk_graddiss/835.

Norwood, Dawn M. 2018. "Conflicted: An Autoethnography on Researching the Minority Swimming Gap." *International Journal of Aquatic Research and Education* 11 (1), article 4. https://doi.org/10.25035/ijare.11.01.04.

Norwood, Dawn M., Steven Waller, and LeQuez Spearman. 2014. "Going Deep: Experiences of a Division I University's First Black Female Competitive Swimmer." *International Journal of Aquatic Research and Education* 8 (3): 258-276. https://doi.org/10.1123/ijare.2013-0034.

Quash, Tiffany Monique. 2018. "Swimming Through the Waves: Black Collegiate Swimmers and Their Experiences." *International Journal of Aquatic Research and Education* 11 (1): 6. https://doi.org/DOI: 10.25035/ijare.11.01.06.

Quash, Tiffany Monique. 2019. "Learning to Swim Is a Human Right." December 2019. Filmed in December 2019 in Bloomington, IN. TED video, 16:56. www.ted.com/talks/tiffany_monique_quash_learning_to_swim_is_a_human_right.

Quash, Tiffany Monique, Knolan C. Rawlins, and Shaun M. Anderson. 2020. "A Comprehensive Analysis of Aquatic Programming at Historically Black Colleges and Universities (HBCUs)." *International Journal of Aquatic Research and Education* 12 (3), article 2.

Walker, Rob. 2021. "'I Was the Only Black Kid in the Pool': Why Swimming Is So White." *Guardian*, April 4, 2021. www.theguardian.com/sport/2021/apr/04/i-was-the-only-black-kid-in-the-pool-why-swimming-is-so-white.

Photo courtesy of Pexel.

# Colorism and Protecting the CROWN

*Tara B. Blackshear*

After five years of teaching experience, Tina Roberts knew many students dreaded outdoor activities. To be honest, she also dreaded the outdoor units and anxiously tossed and turned the night before the first day of the soccer unit. Her physical education (PE) colleagues gave in to student complaints about going outside, but she wanted to give students a well-rounded experience beyond basketball. She reflected, "the hotter outside, the more disgruntled students tend to be," so she made sure there were extra water stations and asked the custodian to bring out the industrial fan where students could huddle during breaks. She also sent a notification email and posted a message on the PE website about the upcoming unit:

Dear students and guardians, tomorrow is the first day of the soccer unit. Please bring a reusable water bottle and a hat or sun visor. Students are allowed to wear sunglasses for outdoor activities, and the PE department provides SPF 30 sunscreen.

Thank you, and I look forward to seeing you on the soccer field!

—Ms. Roberts

Ms. Roberts also had paper cups for students who did not have a water bottle. She worked hard to provide high-quality instruction and set up everything perfectly. She felt ready for the soccer unit and added a few special competitive tasks for her fourth-period class—a competitive group. She hoped her changes would motivate students to engage fully in the soccer unit.

*A group of Black boys laughing*

"Yo mama so black, she went to night school and got marked absent."

*Boys bent over with laughter*

"Yo mama so black, she can leave fingerprints on charcoal."

*Laughter*

"Yo mama so black, she's the reason kids are afraid of the dark."

*Laughter turns to giggles as Ms. Roberts walks toward them*

"I heard what you said about each other's mothers; you need to stop— that's not nice, and there is nothing funny."

*Clarence, still laughing*

"Awww, Ms. Roberts, you don't understand, we are just playin'. It's a Black thing, you wouldn't understand."

Put off by Clarence's response, Ms. Roberts consulted with Mrs. Johnson, a history and science teacher with 20 years at the school, about the jokes some of the Black boys said about Black mothers and how they made her uncomfortable.

Mrs. Johnson wore an Afro, loved and embraced her Blackness, and had developed the mandated Black history curriculum that served as a stand-alone program and was embedded in multiple courses. "Mrs. Johnson, I have several boys in class that make fun of each other's mothers and talk about how Black they are. They said I wouldn't understand because I am white."

Mrs. Johnson shook her head in disgust, because she thought playing the dozens was a thing of the past and firmly believed it needed to stay there. She thought to herself, "these boys must have had a family reunion with old folks." Embarrassed by the notion that they thought it was okay to air Black folks' business at school in front of white teachers, she suspected they were not aware of the historical significance and current implications of these jokes. Equally important, she was concerned with the continued mental trauma on the Black psyche related to hue; she remembers Black girls praying for lighter skin and desiring straight hair. And while these were jokes of the past, she was cognizant that skin tone and messages about "good hair" were deeply rooted in American culture, and unfortunately, did not center Blackness. Proud of the recent progress of the celebration of Black beauty, as shown by Black women wearing natural hairstyles and iconic high-melanin women leads like Viola Davis and Lupita Nyong'o, coupled with a strong resurgence in Black pride generated from the movie *Black Panther*, these derogatory jokes were incredibly painful for Mrs. Johnson, and certainly a setback.

Ms. Roberts said, "Please, Mrs. Johnson, I need your help. I don't know what to do."

Mrs. Johnson replied, "I thought you were woke and knew how to handle Black students. Why are you asking me about Black jokes and issues of colorism if you know everything about teaching Black children?" Mrs. Johnson rolled her eyes and said under her breath but intended for Ms. Roberts' ears, "They always think they know it all but then come running to us when confronted with Black culture."

Mrs. Johnson snapped at Ms. Roberts not only because she was furious with these boys' behavior but also because Ms. Roberts would brag about how "woke" she was when teaching Black children. Her commentary frequently included statements like "I have mastered the art of teaching Black students in PE," and she thought since she lived in a predominantly Black neighborhood and had dated Black men, she earned her honorary "Black card." Mrs. Johnson felt that if Ms. Roberts were so woke, she would not waste her time asking such questions so often.

Ms. Roberts, not familiar with the term "colorism," asked, "What is colorism? I have never heard that word before."

This question further irritated Mrs. Johnson because Ms. Roberts would regularly point out her culturally relevant professional development certifications that hung in her office. Not surprised, Mrs. Johnson responded, "The fact that you have not heard of colorism is telling."

Upon reflection, and after the history lesson (or rather, scolding) she got from Mrs. Johnson about colorism, it dawned on Ms. Roberts why students hated going outside—and it had nothing to do with the heat. She was disappointed in not figuring this out on her own—which should have been apparent since the same students loved indoor soccer. The relationship of darker skin tones to negative health and academic outcomes that Mrs. Johnson shared in her Black history lesson further upset Ms. Roberts, as she realized that she treated darker skin students more harshly than lighter skin students. She noticed a similar pattern among other colleagues—Black and white. In a panic due to this revelation, she felt sick. Needing to do something to minimize the angst she felt, she conducted a quick Google search and entered "colorism." Several pages of content appeared, but there was no time to read because Ms. Roberts had to prepare for the next class. Distracted and deflated, she thought about the collective work she did to meet the needs of her students, including taking a Black history course, purchasing a home in the community, attending teacher trainings, and building student rapport.

That evening, Ms. Roberts went online in search of the history of color-ism and colorism in physical education and sport. She purchased recently published anti-racist books and bookmarked new online resources. Sur-prised that the *Journal of Physical Education Recreation and Dance* (JOPERD) had an article about colorism titled "Understanding Colorism and How it Relates to Sport and Physical Education," she printed the article and read it three times, highlighting several key points. While doing so, she broke down in tears with the reckoning of how she treated certain students and asked herself, "Am I racist? How did I not know these things from all of the anti-racist and culturally relevant teaching workshops I have attended?" Denying the possibility that she could be racist due to the work she put into anti-racist pedagogy, she asked, "Can racism be subconscious?" She conducted another Internet search, "How to tell if you are racist." Results led her to a white fragility test to determine if she was racist, which she took and was saddened by her results. Although troubled by the outcome, she at least had a better understanding of why many Black students, especially the girls, did not want to go outside. She had to examine the assumptions she made about student behaviors during certain physical activities.

Fraught with the understanding that she may have posed harm to stu-dents, Ms. Roberts went into high gear to correct her actions and inaction. She planned and rehearsed her responses for the next time she heard the "yo mama so black" jokes that Clarence and his buddies traded. She put on her vision board her game plan to document negative and positive inter-actions with students for the rest of the semester to make sure her actions were fair and equitable across racial and color lines. Incorporating one of the teaching strategies from the *JOPERD* article, she informed Mrs. Johnson of her plan, seeking approval and validation for her efforts. She wanted Mrs. Johnson to know that she was really trying and was committed to creating a better environment for Black youth.

Despite a bad start to the soccer unit, Ms. Roberts felt better going into the second day after talking to Mrs. Johnson, conducting Internet research the night before, and developing her plan of action.

Clarence: "Yo mama so black—"

Ms. Roberts sharply cut off Clarence before he could continue. "I don't like how you talk negatively about Blackness and the women who birthed you." She continued, "Dark skin tones are beautiful! Why do you think white people bake in the sun for hours just to get a little color?!" Ms. Roberts chuckles. "We have our own beauty extremes, too. Deep down, many of us are envious of naturally dark skin." (While this may be true, Ms. Rob-erts missed the mark by equating envy and suntanning to intracultural anti-Blackness propagated by myths of white superiority and the deleterious effects of colorism.) She noticed a few students with darker complexions smiled cheek to cheek, while other students were tickled. "Y'all hear Ms. Roberts say Blackness?"

*Laughter*

Eboni, a female student with a mahogany complexion present during this exchange, chimed in with conviction, "The blacker the berry, the sweeter the juice! You betta recognize your Black queen mothers! You–need–to–study–your–history, CLARENCE!"

*Class laughter*

Clarence responded in an endearing manner like a big brother talking to a younger sister, "Aww, Eboni, shut up, you know what time it is." Eboni responded with laughter, "Boy, you shut up!"

"Teach him, Eboni! Don't believe everything you think, Clarence," said Jamaal. Jamaal, like Eboni, was in the young scholars club, a strong student in PE, had been accepted into several institutions on an academic scholarship, and had a passion for Black and sport history, "We are told many lies about who and what we are, especially here. KNOW THYSELF!"

Ms. Roberts was about to check Clarence for telling Eboni to "shut up" but remembered what Mrs. Johnson had said about the diverse meanings of certain words, especially when all parties are in agreement. Ms. Roberts decided instead to use this as a teachable moment regarding high melanin versus low melanin. "Clarence and the rest of the class, Eboni has a point. The darker the skin tone, the better protection against the sun's harmful ultraviolet (UV) rays when participating in outdoor activities like soccer, so I expect to see all of you playing hard the remainder of the soccer unit."

© Shutterstock

"Ms. Roberts, melanin don't stop our hair from sweatin' out!"

"My mama spent way too much money on my hair for me to run hard outside in PE."

"I know that's right!"

"Can we stay inside like the other PE classes?"

"Pleeeease."

While these girls pleaded to stay inside, they were the least active group—inside and out.

"Ms. Roberts, I'm workin' on them. I keep tellin' them about the beauty and benefits of rockin' our natural hair and the true meaning of protecting our crowns." Eboni shakes her head at the girls, "Y'all need some deprogramming and some self-lovin'—you *need* to take Mrs. Johnson's Black women's history class." Eboni turned back to the teacher, "Ms. Roberts, that course should be a prerequisite or taken simultaneously with PE. It changed and likely saved my life, or at least extended my life. There is a unit on PE, sport, and physical activity."

Ms. Roberts, a bit confused, pulled Eboni aside after class and asked, "What do you mean by natural hair?"

Eboni responded, "like my hair, and her hair, and hers," as she pointed to a few classmates. "And Mrs. Johnson's and Ms. Parker's." Eboni, her peers, and the teachers had different hairstyles and textures, which further confused Ms. Roberts. She hated to go back to Mrs. Johnson after the last exchange, but Mrs. Johnson was the cultural and historical resource at the school.

Instead of asking Mrs. Johnson about natural hair, she went back to Google that evening and entered 'Black women and natural hair.' The first article that appeared was titled "How Natural Black Hair at Work Became a Civil Rights Issue." Unaware of the amount of policing and navigating that revolved around Black people's hair, Ms. Roberts could not believe that a law, the CROWN (Creating a Respectful and Open World for Natural Hair) Act, was created and mandated in several states to provide protection for Black hair. Protective hairstyles worn by Black women were also new to her. Intrigued and saddened by the content of this article, she continued with her search and came across another article titled "The Struggle of Working Out With Black Girl Hair Is Very Real." This article struck a nerve with Ms. Roberts because it specifically addressed PE, which made her think about some of the behaviors she had witnessed from some of her Black female students but not the Black male students. She truly had no idea—this type of cultural awareness and diversity were not addressed in her undergraduate PE program, and most of the teacher workshops were general and did not focus on Black issues in PE. At this moment, she had an epiphany and finally started to see students for who they were rather than the assumptions made by her, PE standards, and the PE curriculum.

The next day, and to Ms. Roberts' surprise, all of the students were engaged in soccer in a way that she had never seen before. Even the girls who seldom participated put forth the effort. Ecstatic, she pulled out her cell phone to record the class for evidence to share with the other PE teachers who gave up on taking students outdoors.

At the end of class, Ms. Roberts expressed her appreciation for students taking the soccer lesson seriously and provided specific positive feedback to each student in hopes that these behaviors would continue throughout the unit. Heading to the locker room, Eboni, along with her friends, told her, "Ms. Tina, we see you trying," and gave her a wink and a smile as they giggled their way to the locker room.

Elated from this experience and confident in her research and new understandings, Ms. Roberts sprinted to tell Mrs. Johnson about her plan to submit a presentation proposal for the next annual PE conference titled "Hair and the Colorism Effect: Strategies That Help Black Girls Move More in PE."

## Critical Race Study Discourse

1. What assumptions do you think Ms. Roberts made about her students?
2. Define and debate the terms woke, white fragility, and anti-Black racism.
3. Identify the culturally relevant teaching practices used in the case study.
4. Identify racist, anti-Black, and allyship behaviors.
5. Distinguish between performative allyship and authentic allyship. Are you an ally? In what ally behaviors do you engage? If you are not an ally, what prevents you from taking on this role?
6. Define and research the history of colorism. Conduct a comparative analysis of colorism within and across cultural groups—Africans/African Americans, Asians/Asian Americans, Latino/a/ Americans.
7. Research and discuss the history of "the dozens." Discuss the impact of these jokes.
8. Distinguish between high-melanin vs. low-melanin. What are the health benefits and risks associated with high-melanin vs. low-melanin? Think of health holistically.
9. Conduct a comparative analysis on the benefits and limitations of dark-skinned vs. light-skinned Black Americans? Discuss how to dismantle these disparities.

10. How do you think Mrs. Johnson responded to Ms. Roberts' call for validation and acceptance? How do you think Ms. Roberts responded to Eboni's final statement?

11. Read the referenced and cited articles in the case study, and discuss the impact of Black women's hair on health, wealth, employment, self-esteem, and physical activity.

12. Research and identify states that have a CROWN Act. Debate this act.

13. What are your thoughts on white or non-Black people conducting training and workshops that focus on Black people? How do you think Mrs. Johnson responded to Ms. Roberts' presentation proposal? How would you respond?

## References and Suggested Resources

A Long Talk About the Uncomfortable Truth (website). 2021. www.alongtalk.com/

Blackshear, Tara B., and Kelsey Kilmon. 2020. "Natural Hair: A Vital Component to Black Women's Health." *Journal of Racial and Ethnic Health Disparities*. http://doi.10.1007/s40615-020-00922-4.

Dabiri, Emma. 2019. *Don't Touch My Hair*. Allen Lane.

DeMisse, Ewenett. 2020. "The Struggle of Working Out With Black Girl Hair Is Very Real." *Femmestella*. September 18, 2020. www.femestella.com/how-black-girl-hair-prevents-black-girls-from-working-out/.

ElObeid, Adila Salih, Afaf Kamal-Eldin, Mohamed Anwar K. Abdelhalim, and Adil M. Haseeb. 2017. "Pharmacological Properties of Melanin and Its Function in Health." *Basic Clinical Pharmacology & Toxicology* 120 (6): 515-522. https://doi.org/10.1111/bcpt.12748.

Flintoff, Anne, Fiona Dowling, and Hayley Fitzgerald. 2021. "Working Through Whiteness, Race and (Anti) Racism in Physical Education Teacher Education." *Physical Education and Sport Pedagogy* 20 (5): 559-570. https://doi.org/10.1080/1740 8989.2014.962017.

Forster-Scott, Latisha. 2013. Understanding Colorism and How it Relates to Sport and Physical Education. *Journal of Physical Education, Recreation & Dance* 82 (2): 48-52. https://doi.org/10.1080.0703084.2011.10598583.

Fulwood III, Sam. 2011. "Playing the Dozens: President Obama Ignores Schoolyard Taunts From Jealous Professor." *Center for American Progress Race and Ethnicity*. ww.americanprogress.org/issues/race/news/2011/05/24/9622/race-and-beyond-playing-the-dozens/.

Golash-Boza, Tanya Maria. 2015. *Race & Racisms: A Critical Approach*. New York: Oxford University Press. https://global.oup.com/us/companion.web-sites/9780199920013/student/ch5/quiz/.

Jokes4us. 2021. "Yo Mama So Black Jokes." Jokes4us.com.

Keith, Verna M., and Carla R. Monroe. 2016. "Histories of Colorism and Implications for Education." *Theory Into Practice* 55 (1): 4-10. https://doi.org/10.1080/0040 5841.2016.1116847.

Lewis, Gregory. 1994. Dozens Is Oral Legacy Rooted in Survival. *Baltimore Sun.* February 14, 1994. www.baltimoresun.com/news/bs-xpm-1994-02-11-1994042244-story.html.

Loewen, James W. 2018. *Lies My Teacher Told Me: Everything Your American History Textbook Got Wrong.* New York: Touchstone.

Miller, Lisa A., and Victor W. Harris. 2018. "I Can't Be Racist—I Teach in an Urban School, and I'm a Nice White Lady!" *World Journal of Education* 8 (3): 1-11. https://files.eric.ed.gov/fulltext/EJ1182572.pdf.

Morrison, Toni. 2007. *The Bluest Eye.* New York: Vintage.

Solano, Francisco. 2020. "Photoprotection and Skin Pigmentation: Melanin-Related Molecules and Some Other New Agents Obtained From Natural Sources." *Molecules* (Basel, Switzerland) 25 (7): 1537. https://doi.org/10.3390/molecules25071537.

Thurman, Wallace. 1929. *The Blacker the Berry the Sweeter the Juice.* Mineola, NY: Dover Publications.

© Shutterstock

# 5

# "Nigga Under the Microscope": Crucial Conflict or Context-Specific?

*Angela K. Beale-Tawfeeq and Yvette Onofre*

Maria, a 25-year-old Latina and recent graduate from Columbia University, is a second-year health and physical education teacher at A.B.L.L.E. (All Black and Latino Learners Excel). A Title I charter high school, A.B.L.L.E. is located in Brooklyn, New York. The demographic snapshot of A.B.L.L.E. reflects a student population of 63 percent African American and 37 percent Latino/a with an economic need index of 72 percent. Forty percent of the students are eligible for free or reduced lunch, and 17 percent are limited English proficiency. There is an 88 percent annual attendance rate, a 66 percent graduation rate, and an annual teacher turnover rate of 10 percent.

Maria finds value as an educator, knowing that her purpose to create change through social justice and equity is supported by not only the Centers for Disease Control and Prevention's announcement of "racism as a public health issue" but also by a recent statement from the Association of Schools and Programs of Public Health on racism and public health, which reads as follows:

America faces three major crises right now, a viral pandemic the likes of which we have not seen since 1918, an economic collapse the likes of which we have not seen since 1932 at the onset of the Great Depression, and the ongoing struggle of civil rights and equity, the likes of which we have not seen since 1968. These are synergistic conditions, which in tandem have enormous implications for public health. And, sadly, they all expose the continuing problem of injustice, inequality, and structural and systemic racism in America.

As she reflects on this information, she decides there is not only a need for public healing but also an opportunity to arm her students with adequate life survival skills via the health and physical activity program, where she strives to create positive character development and moral reasoning. Maria views herself as a liberal, socially conscious agent of change, ready to create quality health and physical education (HPE) programs in underserved communities to serve at-risk Black and Brown youth. Maria first took an interest in youth development and making a difference in children's lives through physical activity when she learned about the teaching for personal and social responsibility (TPSR) model in her K-12 HPE curriculum course. With a focus on sports-based youth development, Maria designs courses to establish an educational environment that supports the social-emotional development of students through the creation of physical education experiences that foster respect, care, and responsibility—pillars of TPSR.

With a backdrop of COVID-19, the social unrest raised around the murder of George Floyd and other African Americans killed by white police officers, the rise of the Black Lives Matter movement, the insurrection attack on the Capitol on January 6, 2021, and the exposure of structural racism and hatred in America, she shepherds students into her physical education classes with care. Daily lessons are grounded in the levels of TPSR:

Level 1: respecting the rights and feelings of others

Level 2: self-motivation

Level 3: self-direction

Level 4: caring and leadership

Level 5: transference

Through structured lessons with the TPSR framework (i.e., relational time, awareness talks, lesson focus, group meetings, reflection time, and the dismissal), she creates a safe and secure educational environment. Maria takes pride in designing nontraditional physical activities and fosters learning experiences that promote social-emotional health and wellness. All students receive cultural, moral, and educational guidance through physical activity and a positive educational environment.

In class, Maria often hears students interact with each other with personal greetings such as "What up, my nigga?," "Yo, that shit is dope, my nigga," and "Nigga, please, I love doing sport yoga," greetings that do not bother her. A fan of hip-hop and always hoping to connect with students, Maria privately listens to Jay-Z and other artists and occasionally recounts a few lyrics to impress students. She gets a rush of happiness when students say, "Ms. Maria knows how to spit some rhymes." On weekends, she blasts "The Story of O.J." and raps alongside Jay-Z, with Spanish flare as if she were on stage. To view the lyrics to Jay-Z's "The Story of O.J.," do an Internet search on these key words: *Lyrics to Jay-Z's "The Story of O.J."*

She loves working out to this song and the freedom she feels when listening to hip-hop music. She is a little jealous that her students can publicly rhyme these verses. Often, Maria justifies to herself that she should be able to say what she wants, especially if she is just repeating what someone else is saying, because she is also a woman of color. Maria has no understanding of the meanings behind the "nigga" variations used by Jay-Z. Furthermore, she is too young to remember the flak J. Lo got for putting "nigga" in her song "I'm Real" over 20 years ago.

Able to connect with students, Maria prides herself on creating an environment where students can engage with her on a personal level. She gives students the freedom to be their authentic selves. As students enter the gym, sharing their normal pleasantries and gathering equipment, Maria focuses her attention on a new student, Bashir. Maria finds Bashir elusive but wants to build a relationship with him to make his transition to a new school smooth. She hopes to connect with him as she does with the other students. Maria wants him to feel that he can trust her and that her class is a safe space.

New to A.B.L.L.E., Bashir is an African American 14-year-old boy in the ninth grade. He recently moved with his family to Brooklyn from Queens. Bashir is the eldest son of four children. Sage (16) is his older sister, and he has two brothers, Jibril (10) and Isa (3 months). Bashir is fortunate to have both parents at home. His mother is a former teacher, now a stay-at-home mom, and his father is a math teacher at a local elementary school. Bashir grew up in Fresh Meadows, Queens, and is an avid baseball player. His mother is a proud woman and always reminds him of the importance of cultural awareness and history, especially to an African American male, and there is the understanding that his father is the *griot* of the family. In West Africa, the griot is a leader, historian, and keeper of the oral tradition for a community, a wise man. To Bashir, his dad is a wise man and the family's protector.

The move to Brooklyn was sudden, due to his *emayay's* (grandmother's) hospital stay. The family learned that she tested positive for COVID-19. To Bashir, family is everything, with his emayay as the cornerstone. Since her diagnosis, Bashir has been remembering the stories his father and emayay would tell him about growing up during de jure segregation and the civil rights periods. His father has often told stories of Emayay growing up in Winnsboro, South Carolina, and the courage that it took for her to come to New York in the 1950s with only a sixth-grade education and her name. Names are important; as Emayay always says, "When a name is given to a child, it should mean something, be something to live up to, because the power of the spoken word can make or break a man."

One day, the family was listening and singing along to Jay-Z's "Empire State of Mind." To view the lyrics to Jay-Z's "Empire State of Mind," do an Internet search on these key words: *Lyrics to Jay-Z's "Empire State of Mind."*

Emayay shouted "Turn that off!" Everyone immediately turned to respond, as one does when an elder speaks. "Did you hear that word?!"

"What word, Emayay?" Bashir asked. "Jay-Z says a lot of words."

Emayay, 80 years old, turned toward Bashir and responded, "*Nigga*? Why would he think it is okay to say such a word to describe himself or someone else?"

Bashir looked respectfully and lovingly in Emayay's eyes and used his favorite saying, "'cause I'm built different," and with a laugh continued, "Oh it's only a word, Emayay, and everybody says it."

"Well, do you know what it means?" asked Emayay.

"Yes, I know what it means. It's a bad word used in history to disrespect us, African Americans, but in our culture, it also can mean that's my friend, my brother, my man," Bashir confidently said. Bashir continued, "Emayay, it doesn't matter what it used to mean, we have taken the power back by taking off the '-er' that was placed to hurt us and say that we aren't human. By adding the '-a,' we are saying yes-we-are and more."

Emayay paused, lovingly hugged and smiled at Bashir, and said, "Let's sit down." After sitting, Emayay looked at Bashir and continued, "My love, I understand and hear you, but I think it is more. What I want you to remember is the word *nigga* is rooted in hatred and anger, no matter how it is spelled. Hatred and death still are a part of the spoken word *nigga*. It gives power to make people pause, question the meaning and the intention of the person saying it." Emayay continued, "The origins of the word *nigga* come from the Latin word *niger*, meaning black, a beautiful color that envelops all of the colors that God created. And that feeling of power and respect, Bashir, is what I always want you to embrace." Bashir lowered his head. Emayay, in her loving and proud way, held both sides of his face, lifted his head, and spoke again, "Bashir, it is within this light that you and your siblings received your names: Bashir, meaning 'a good word'; Sage, meaning 'wisdom'; Jibril, meaning 'bringer of a good word'; and Isa, meaning 'Jesus, son of God' and 'God is my oath.' My Bashir, embrace the strength of your heritage and our people to survive and exist. Be strong, be respected, be acknowledged. Loved and live. And never forget that to be called or acknowledged by any other name like *nigga* is a loss of your power—power that is only yours to give."

These words and feelings enveloped Bashir and have provided comfort since arriving at A.B.L.L.E. Bashir appreciates the camaraderie and the efforts taken to build a school whose mission is to build a community where students can learn and grow—a big change from P.S. 26 in Queens. His favorite class is physical education, and he enjoys learning about TPSR and the way that physical education allows students to communicate with each other and Ms. Maria while getting fit. He is particularly excited about the new unit of sport yoga. Ms. Maria tells them about the focus on mental and emotional health—an objective for the unit. Bashir wants to use sport yoga to learn how to focus on his mental preparation and flexibility for baseball. He hopes to make the baseball team this year.

As a new student, he doesn't know a lot of his classmates. In Ms. Maria's class, he likes how students get to build relationships and talk about the way their day is going during relational time. He also appreciates how Ms. Maria supports students to talk about the importance of self-respect, effort, and responsibility during the awareness talk, group meeting, and reflection time. To be authentic and create and establish valuable and caring friendships makes him believe that his "new kid" status will not be so bad. Although he does not say much to anyone, Bashir, for the first time in a class of 30 students, does not feel like he is out of place.

In fact, the ability to establish meaningful relationships is why Bashir thinks Ms. Maria is a great teacher and why he enjoys physical education. Often during relational time or group meetings, Bashir hear and sees how Ms. Maria welcomes all students and allows students to be themselves, letting them say things like "Yo, that shit is dope, my nigga" and "Nigga, please, I love doing sport yoga." Although choosing not to say the word, he understands how and why his classmates used the word. He remembers what Emayay told him about power and pride.

But today, when Bashir enters the gym and students are sharing their normal exchanges, Ms. Maria greets him with a high five and says, "What up, my nigga?" Bashir stops and looks at her.

Will their relationship ever be the same?

## Critical Race Study Discourse

1. What do you think is going through Bashir's mind when Ms. Maria greets him with a high five and says, "What up, my nigga?" What do you think Bashir should do?

2. What do you think is going through Maria's mind when she greets Bashir with a high five and says, "What up, my nigga?"

How do you think that her professional behavior aligns with her teaching philosophy and expected student outcomes?

3. Is Maria's behavior ever acceptable? Why or why not?

4. With restorative practices, empowerment, and education being key elements within the mission of the school, what role should administrators have to ensure that educators are prepared to model this philosophy within the classroom and school?

5. How can Maria build empathy for Bashir and repair the harm she may have caused as a result of her use of the word *nigga*?

6. Do you think that Maria should be so concerned about establishing a relationship with Bashir, one student, rather than having relationships and being a role model for all students?

7. What would you do if you heard your students using the word *nigga*? Does the ethnicity of the students make a difference in the permissions or acceptability of using the term *nigga* within the educational environment? Why or why not? Do you think that it is okay for students to use the word *nigga*? Please explain.

8. What do you think needs to happen to make things right between Bashir and Maria? Consider all stakeholders (i.e., students, parents, administrators, and teachers).

9. Do you think language is important? The term *nigga* is traumatic because of its historical use. How do you think teachers should address the reality of student collective trauma?

## References and Suggested Resources

Asim, Jabari. 2007. *The N Word: Who Can Say it, Who Shouldn't, and Why*. Boston: Houghton Mifflin.

Association of Schools and Programs of Public Health (ASPPH). "ASPPH Statement: Racism Is a Public Health Crisis." https://s3.us-east-1.amazonaws.com/ASPPH_Media_Files/Docs/Final%20ASPPH%20Statement%20on%20racism.pdf (accessed August 31, 2020).

Beale, Angela. 2016. "Making a Difference: TPSR, a New Wave of Youth Development Changing Lives One Stroke at a Time." *Journal of Physical Education, Recreation & Dance* 87 (5): 31-34.

Fisher, Ericka J. 2008. "The N-Word: Reducing Verbal Pollution in Schools." *The Clearing House: A Journal of Educational Strategies, Issues and Ideas* 81 (6): 278-281. https://doi.org/10.3200/TCHS.81.6.278-281.

Flaherty, Colleen. 2020. "Professor Apologizes for Using the N-Word." *Inside Higher Ed*, May 13, 2020. www.insidehighered.com/quicktakes/2020/05/13/professor-apologizes-using-n-word.

Martinek, Tom, and Don Hellison. 2016. "Learning Responsibility Through Sport and Physical Activity." In *Positive Youth Development Through Sport*, edited by N.L. Holt, 180-190. New York: Routledge.

Rahman, Jacquelyn. 2012. "The N Word: Its History and Use in the African American Community." *Journal of English Linguistics* 40 (2): 137-171. https://doi.org/10.1177/0075424211414807.

Reiter, Bernd. 2018. "The Griots of West Africa: Oral Tradition and Ancestral Knowledge." In *Constructing the Pluriverse: The Geopolitics of Knowledge*. Durham, NC: Duke University Press.

Sullivan, Rachel E. 2003. "Rap and Race: It's Got a Nice Beat, but What About the Message?" *Journal of Black Studies* 33 (5): 605-622. www.jstor.org/stable/3180978.

Walsh, David S., Jimmy Ozaeta, and Paul M. Wright. 2010. "Transference of Responsibility Model Goals to the School Environment: Exploring the Impact of a Coaching Club Program." *Physical Education and Sport Pedagogy* 15 (1): 15-28. https://doi.org/10.1080/17408980802401252.

Warftosky, Alona. 2001. "Protestors See No Affection in J. Lo's Use of Racial Epithet." *Washington Post*, July 14, 2001. www.washingtonpost.com/archive/lifestyle/2001/07/14/protesters-see-no-affection-in-jlos-use-of-racial-epithet/2b9832d0-6275-4cb6-b1b2-6bb990f2745b.

© Shutterstock

# 6

# Black, Male, Queer, Athletic, and Academically Gifted

*Tara B. Blackshear, Afi C. Blackshear, and Akinyemi K. Blackshear*

Bo Stevens, the up-and-coming quintessential physical educator, debunked stereotypic portrayals of the dumb sports jock turned gym teacher narrative often depicted in movies. With his muscular, athletic stature combined with intelligence, enthusiasm, planning, and authentic assessment capabilities, Bo could elevate physical education by serving as a role model for the field. Described as the "total package," Bo was highly sought after by principals in the area, and his letters of recommendation from university faculty were outstanding. His diversity and inclusion statement was compelling: He had earned an athletic scholarship and played Division I football at a historically Black institution (HBI). He described his experiences as a minority, given that only 5 percent of the team was white, and white students were only 2 percent of the student body.

Strategic in his university choice but publicly failing to acknowledge that he benefited from affirmative action, Bo tells his friends, "I got affirmative-actioned by a Black player who took my spot" at his top choice school—the only neighboring historically white institution with a football team and physical education (PE) program. The experience attending an HBI, however, served Bo well. He became aware of the diverse cultural nuances among Black people, which he exploited during his job applications and interviews. The Movement for Black Lives was prominent during this time, and talks of authentic methods of addressing diversity, equity, and inclusion were finally making it to the educational mainstream.

During his interviews, Bo captivated every principal with his responses to how he ensures equity among all students. Principals and athletic directors debated why their school was a good fit and tried to barter to secure Bo, especially schools with large percentages of Black male students and strong football programs. Given Bo's HBI experience, he was an ideal candidate who could relate to all students.

Comfortable with Black people and wanting a head football coaching position, Bo accepted a job offer at Dr. Martin Luther King Jr. High School (MLK), where the head football coach had recently retired. Opportunities for a head football coaching position are rare for first-year teachers, but Bo and the principal were confident and believed in his ability. Snide remarks surfaced that Bo got the job through affirmative action, because there were only a handful of white male teachers at MLK. Coach Randy Hopkins, one of the assistant football coaches and fellow physical educators, had been at the school for 10 years. Promised the head coaching job, Coach Hopkins was upset and suspected that Bo and the principal bonded through their stereotypic views of manhood—that "good ol' boy" tendencies solidified Bo's position. Coach Hopkins, however, did not hold this against Bo, because his commitment to students and the football program was his priority.

Since football is a first-season sport, Bo started early for preseason planning and recruitment to build rapport with the assistant coaches and current players. Principal John Edwards introduced Bo to Randy and the team captains from last season—Tyrell Johnson (folks called him "T.J.") and Mike. They exchanged the traditional football greeting, but T.J. looked at Bo with familiarity and asked, "Have we met? Do I know you from somewhere?"

Bo responded self-consciously, thinking about his diverse circle of friends and acquaintances, "I don't think so." T.J. was certain he knew Bo but could not put his finger on it—he never forgot a face. Bo followed up, "Did you attend football camp at Morgan State University? Maybe that's where you saw me."

T.J. replied, "Nah, I went to camp at University of Maryland."

T.J., whose interests were well rounded, was the school's renaissance man. He was athletic, he played the cello, he was liked by most fellow students, and he had his pick of universities to attend. T.J. openly identified as queer and had always had the freedom to be authentic at home, at school, and around teammates. He was fortunate that he was not forced into the "down-low" culture that plagues many Black men afraid to escape narrow views of Black masculinity and sexuality. Mike, also intelligent, athletic, and well rounded, was best friends with T.J. Their parents were college friends and had purchased homes on the same block when the boys were two. They grew up like brothers and were considering attending the same university. Mike also challenged perceptions of Black masculinity by taking and excelling in dance every year, as did T.J. by playing football as an openly gay player.

Principal Edwards shared a few details with Bo about the boys, including T.J.'s sexuality. He said, "You know T.J. bats for the other team" in Randy's presence, which infuriated him.

Randy, a queer-straight alliance board member, instantly reacted, saying, "What the hell does T.J.'s sexuality have to do with this conversation? You have no idea who you might offend!"

Mr. Edwards quickly tried to defuse the situation, "I didn't mean any harm, but T.J. doesn't act or look gay, so I thought Bo should know."

Randy replied, "And what does that mean, Mr. Edwards? Tell me, what does gay look like?" Mr. Edwards, afraid of confrontation, left abruptly, indicating that he had a meeting in a few minutes. Bo told Randy that everything was "all good" and that he had no problem with T.J.

T.J. and Mike made plans to reach out to players via social media. While posting, T.J. told Mike, "I know Coach Stevens but can't remember how or where."

Mike said, "I can't believe he got the job over Coach Hopkins. I was looking forward to having a Black head coach senior year."

T.J. replied, "Yeah, that's some bullllllshit."

T.J. and Mike had been with Coach Hopkins since ninth-grade PE and had taken courses from him in grades 10 and 11. They were also enrolled for his class in grade 12. He was their first PE teacher who kept the "E" in PE and got them both interested in studying biomechanics after taking the International Baccalaureate sports, exercise, and health science course that he taught. It was in ninth-grade PE, however, that Coach Hopkins recognized T.J. as a star student and potential football player. He encouraged T.J. to try out for the team.

Coach Hopkins, a straight Black man, was a vocal ally for queer students—unusual, because many Black men have been raised since times of colonialism and enslavement in environments of toxic masculinity. These ideas have been packaged and disseminated in schools, churches, and the media. Coach Hopkins has received several teaching awards and has been instrumental in establishing the school's inclusive culture through his reputation for speaking truth to power, so it was easy for T.J. to consider trying out for the team.

T.J. said, "I bet Coach Hopkins speaking up for queer students and calling out injustices is why he is not the coach."

"Maybe, but he *is* a Black man at the end of the day, and Coach Hopkins doesn't 'know his place.' He obviously got overlooked for the inexperienced white guy. You know this happens all the time. Look at college football and the NFL. We are good enough to run on the athletic plantation but not good enough to lead or have ownership."

T.J. looked thoughtful. "I have a bad feeling about him, too. I *know* I know him from somewhere."

Mike said, "We should look him up."

The boys looked for Bo Stevens online. With surprising ease, they came across a Twitter profile, @Boss, with a profile photo that appeared to be Bo Stevens grimacing with sunglasses and a baseball cap. In response to an NFL player coming out, @Boss tweeted "Faggots don't belong on the field, they belong in hell," and when players were kneeling during the national anthem at NFL games, @Boss tweeted, "These Blacks don't know how good they got it. Stand up, shut up, and play the game."

After scrolling further, T.J. then saw the following exchange between himself and @Boss from when the rapper, Lil Nas X, released his music video for "Montero." A tweet @Boss wrote about Lil Nas X generated a lot of interaction. "After that gay-ass video, Lil Nas X should change his name to Lil queer nigger. The world praising men like this is what is wrong with our society." T.J. immediately recognized this tweet because he had responded with a photo of Lil Nas X.

Tweet: @Boss "can any of my black brothas out there put Lil Nas X in his place *laugh emoji* *puke emoji* [reply from @Boss] i dont care, ya'll can act like im wrong. no man, especially black ones, supposed to dance like that. you all can hate, i know my heart, im down with the community. *fist emoji* *fist emoji* *puke emoji* *cry laugh emoji*"

@TJ_Plays_Games replied, "Shut up, fool. Ratio this homophobe with Lil Nas X."

But that interaction was hardly the worst of it. Bo Stevens' Twitter feed was littered with tweets condescending and degrading women, members of the LGBTQ+ community, Black people, and people of color, generally.

"I knew it! I knew he looked familiar." T.J.'s tweet had ultimately "ratio'd" Bo's, gaining over 2,000 likes and more retweets than Bo's. This meant that T.J. still received notifications from it, which broadcast Bo's Twitter picture on T.J.'s feed with each interaction, again and again.

After processing for a moment, Mike asked, "The school must not know, huh?"

"Dude, he went to an HBI. You see how they touted Coach Stevens around like he was the next unifier because of it, and you *know* that's probably where their search started and stopped."

Mike's eyes were glued to the screen. He wasn't surprised. People's true thoughts and values show when they think they have the anonymity of the Internet to hide behind, but at the same time, he couldn't believe it. "Only a white guy. If he were Black, they would have done every background check and would have found at least 30 different reasons not to hire him at all in the first five tweets alone."

During practice, T.J. often felt Coach Stevens' eyes gaze over his body—not in an "I am interested in you" kind of way but in a perplexed manner. T.J. wondered if Coach Stevens remembered the Twitter exchange they had. It didn't matter if @Boss deleted the content because he knew they had the receipts.

Alone with Mike, Coach Stevens asked, "Are you sure you aren't on the down-low? You spend a lot of time with T.J., and you dance better than the other boys in class. You hold your hands a certain way, too. I know a thing or two about this after my time at MSU—you can trust me. It's funny, you and T.J. could switch status. He's uber-masculine and does not fit the mold—athletic, smart, articulate, and sociable—not typical." Mike stares at him, angry but silent from disbelief. He later tells his parents and T.J. about the incident.

In the first game of the season, T.J. and Mike took a knee during the national anthem. Most people probably thought they were reinstating Colin Kaepernick's racial injustice protest, but they were protesting Coach Stevens' homophobic and racist behaviors and the fact that the real quintessential teacher-coach, ally, and Black man was overlooked. They were willing to give up their positions to do the right thing and had their parents' approval. Bo angrily confronted them, realizing he needed to save face, "If you two don't get off your knees, you won't play!" T.J. and Mike did not budge and looked Bo in the eyes as the national anthem ended.

Bo kept his threat and did not play the two best players on the team, which cost them a loss against one of their toughest rivals. He also blew the school's record of three years undefeated, and the crowd, T.J., and Mike's parents let Bo know that he had made a huge mistake. Bo, upset and frustrated at the loss, told T.J. and Mike that he would bench them all season if he had to. T.J. and Mike were unfazed. They had the upper hand with the information they had on Coach Stevens, and at the end of the game, with a smirk, T.J. said, "We know who you are, @Boss," and smiled as they walked off the field to greet their parents. Bo looked terrified because his private identity was known.

Over the weekend, T.J. and Mike emailed the tweet storm to the local news station to make sure Coach Stevens' actions were not swept under the rug. The school district claimed they were anti-racist, LGBTQIA+ allies, and an overall inclusive place, but there were many stories where Mr. Edwards and the school district refused to take action and found a way to further victimize the students. Mr. Edwards and the district had the facade of equity, but their (in)actions spoke volumes.

On Monday, Principal Edwards called T.J. and Mike to his office, pulling them out of Coach Hopkins' weight training class. He berated and lectured them about their disrespectful behavior and how Bo deserved respect. "Go easy on Coach Stevens, he is a first-year teacher and a white head coach at a predominantly Black school and needs to be given a chance."

Twitter exchange between @Boss and T.J.

Fabricated tweets inspired by real events, but they are not real.

© Shutterstock

Interrupting Principal Edwards' verbal lashing, T.J. took out his phone and showed Mr. Edwards @Boss' tweets just as channel 7 reporters pressed up against Mr. Edwards' office door with cameras flashing and a barrage of questions.

## Critical Race Study Discourse

1. Research and discuss the sexuality continuum. Distinguish and discuss racialized LGBTQIA+ stereotypes. Examine the "down-low" phenomenon and its impact on the Black community. What are the factors that keep some Black gay men in the closet? How can we eliminate these factors? Research the outcomes when Black male students and athletes reveal that they are gay or not heterosexual?

2. Historically, queer had a negative connotation. Research the history of queer and analyze the transformation of the term. Distinguish the evolutions of queer and the n-word.

3. Research affirmative action and identify who mostly benefits? Do perceptions match reality? How do you feel about affirmative action? Debate affirmative action. Suggest, create or identify equitable hiring policies.

4. Distinguish Black Lives Matter and the Movement for Black Lives.

## References and Suggested Resources

Anderson, Eric, and Mark McCormack. 2010. "Comparing the Black and Gay Male Athlete: Patterns in American Oppression." *Journal of Men's Studies* 18 (2): 145-158. https://doi.org/10.3149/jms.1802.145.

Anderson, Eric, and Mark McCormack. 2010. "Intersectionality, Critical Race Theory, and American Sporting Oppression: Examining Black and Gay Male Athletes." *Journal of Homosexuality* 57 (8): 949-967. https://doi.org/10.1080/00918369.2010.503502.

Boykin, Keith. 2005. *Beyond the Down Low: Sex and Denial in Black America*. New York: Carroll & Graf.

Buzinski, J. 2020. "A Conversation With T.J. Callan About the History of Gay Black Men Coming Out in Sports." *SB Nation Out Sports*, March 3, 2020. www.outsports.com/2020/3/3/21154009/tj-callan-gay-black-athletes-michael-sam-jason-collins.

Carrington, Ben. 1998. "Sport, Masculinity, and Black Cultural Resistance." *Journal of Sport & Social Issues* 22 (3): 275-298. https://doi.org/10.1177/019372398022003004.

Glenn, Cerise, and Andrew Spieldenner. 2013. "An Intersectional Analysis of Television Narratives of African American Women with African American Men on 'the Down Low.'" *Sexuality & Culture* 17 (3): 401-416. https://doi.org/10.1007/s12119-013-9189-y.

Movement for Black Lives. 2021. https://m4bl.org/

Sewell, Christopher. 2020. "Finding Lionel: Reconciling Multiple Identities as Black, Gay, and Gifted in *Dear White People*." *Taboo: The Journal of Culture & Education* 19 (1): 30-50.

© Shutterstock

# More Than a Bathroom: Black Transgender Student

*Tiffany Monique Quash*

As a child, Star Edmonds knew she was unlike the other girls in her school. She grew up in a primarily Black neighborhood and has known everyone in her community since the day she was born. In fact, it was the same neighborhood where her parents met each other as children, and they continued to live there when they returned from college. Star's parents are workaholics but always make time for Star and her brother Benjamin, who is two years older. Star's mother, Debra, is a professor at the local university and coaches soccer on the weekend. Her father, James, is a math teacher at the local high school and coaches swimming. Athletics are important for the family, as well as having dinner together and being present for all soccer games and swim meets. Her family focuses on family, grades, community, and athletics (not always in this order). So, you can only imagine the reaction when this humble family's second child said to them at the tender age of five that her outsides did not match how she felt on the inside.

This case study was written by a self-identified cisgender Black queer womxn. Though I am not a part of the transgender community, this case is an attempt to respectfully address the challenges of one nonfictional Black transgender girl based on numerous conversations and experiences. It is the intention of this chapter to honor the silenced voices of my transgender siblings.

Star was assigned male at birth and began objecting to the clothes chosen, books read, and the pronouns used early on. At first, Debra and James thought that this was a phase. For example, the first words from Star were screaming and crying "no's" when James was dressing her in stereotypical boy clothes. Then, she wanted only unicorns and rainbows in her room and started throwing her brother's toys out of her room. Although this could happen with any child who has any aversion to certain objects, that was not the case for Star. When she was five, Debra and James decided to no longer use Star's dead name and to allow her to choose her name, clothes, books, and toys. The reason Star chose the name "Star" was that she always felt that she was uniquely different from everyone else. Hence, she was a . . . Star!

Over the years, Debra and James emotionally and psychologically prepared their family for what could come by reaching out to therapists to discuss what they could expect. Through this journey, they each realized that they would dedicate themselves to learning about their internal biases, which would require time, work, energy, love, and forgiveness. Debra acknowledged that she felt that she lost her second child through this process and cried many nights, blaming herself. James became angry that he no longer had this son. They both mourned with each other and continued ongoing healing through therapy. Finally, there came the point of asking for forgiveness from Star.

Unlike their parents, Benjamin felt that as the older sibling, he was always meant to protect Star. Over the years, he felt that much of the attention had gone toward Star instead of them both. Benjamin managed to acknowledge his own resentment and spoke with their parents candidly about his feelings. The family recognized the conscious effort needed to reprogram their thoughts and behaviors that had been developed culturally through upbringing and environmentally through learned behaviors. Most importantly, the need for open communication became a functioning factor for the emotional wellness of the family.

The Edmonds family got through the beginning stages of Star's transition, starting with what could be said and heard. The community they lived in was not as forgiving. Many of the neighborhood kids refused to come over to the Edmonds house for playdates. Benjamin experienced bullying from his teammates during practices and game days. During practice, one of Benjamin's teammates yelled, "Don't pass the ball to Ben, you may catch what his faggoty ass *brother* has!" Debra was the coach for Benjamin's team, and parents were going behind her back to speak with league officials to see if she could be removed as head coach. Nothing went smoothly for the Edmonds family. Over time, friends, and even some family members, decided to no longer speak with them, but the Edmonds family persevered.

In grade school, Star's and Benjamin's school experiences were intolerable for the family. The bullying that occurred in the public school would infiltrate the soccer field or the swimming pool and vice versa. Teachers were unwilling to understand Star or listen to her parents' concerns. The classroom became a battleground. The family encountered strong resistance, such as

- assertions that "what is written on the birth certificate should be said on the first day,"
- false child abuse claims by teachers,
- accusations of enabling a minor to wear inappropriate clothes to school, and
- adults challenging the minor's mental capacity to make sound decisions.

On the pool deck, some parents were afraid that something would happen in the bathroom if Star walked into the girl's bathroom prior to a swim meet. Rather than deal with patronizing parents and swim meet directors, Star changed into her bathing suit at home and arrived prepared for warm-up prior to the meet. Every part of the Edmonds' day was methodically planned in advance.

After four schools (both private and public) and, eventually, a move 20 minutes from their lifelong neighborhood, the Edmonds family finally found a match that could last until high school. The private school educational experience was a financial burden and was far less diverse. Everyone knew private school was a temporary fix for Star until she could join her brother at the high school. With a change of scenery for the family, there was hope that this new home and neighborhood would be a part of the solution toward Star and Benjamin's educational experience.

## The First Day

In preparation for each school year, Debra, James, Benjamin, and Star would meet with all the teachers, guidance counselors, principals, and coaches ahead of time to address the "name issues" and which correct pronouns to use. At the beginning of ninth grade for Star, her physical education teacher, Mr. Victor Jones, didn't attend this meeting. Mr. Jones was also head swim coach for the high school. Mr. Jones was a Black man who professed belief in the church and old-fashioned gender roles. He only respected straight men in leadership roles; he believed women are better seen and not heard, that boys should only play sports where they could get dirty, and that girls should play sports that have little to no dirt involved. As a swim coach, Mr. Jones vocalized his views about discouraging boys from swimming and diving. Over the years, his perspective had broadened slightly, upon seeing that the world idolizes Black male swimmers like Cullen Jones and Reece Whitley. However, Mr. Jones' absence from the meeting concerned the Edmonds family.

Mr. Jones' athletic record was impeccable. The girls' swimming and diving teams ranked first in the state, and his physical education classes were known to be the most challenging. Every athlete enrolled in one of his multiple physical education courses during their four years of attending DuBois High School. Mr. Jones had one rule: "No boys in the girls' class, and no girls in the boys' class." This was the motto that he placed on his office door. Mr. Jones once chided a gay Black male student: "We don't allow a sissy in weightlifting. Go report to the guidance counselor to have your schedule changed to creative writing." Because of Mr. Jones' athletic reputation, this incident (like many others) was never reported to the administration. Even though teachers and administrators were aware there were incidents, they wouldn't take corrective action unless a student's family came forward.

When the first day of high school arrived for Star, everyone knew that high school life was going to be different. Benjamin was going into his third year and was excelling in soccer. The same was going for Star in swimming. Her parents and the other supportive parents at her local club team had approved guidelines that enabled her to swim in a suit in which she felt comfortable and to use her chosen name.

Star was certainly in a different experience navigating high school and the demands of swimming at another level. DuBois High was more ethnically and racially diverse. There were student organizations centered on racial and ethnic interests, drama, debate, newspaper, yearbook, and a gay-straight alliance (GSA). Two years ago, Benjamin transferred to this school for educational and recruitment purposes. Star wanted to do the same, to focus on her education and to be seen by Division I colleges and universities. The parent–teacher conference the week before was a healthy start for the beginning of the new year for Star, but Mr. Jones' absence raised her anxiety in preparation for the first day of physical education and practice.

Star saw starting high school as a fresh start. Despite knowing that it was possible that some of the neighborhood kids attended this school, Star remained optimistic. She spent the night before hoping that she would get a clean slate, going over her class schedule, and thinking about possible scenarios that could come up for her. The biggest challenge would be changing for PE, which was fifth period. Luckily for Star, swim practice immediately followed fifth period, and during the meeting with school personnel, including the nurse, they settled that clothing changes would take place in the nurse's office. Star and her parents agreed that she would use the nurse's bathroom for the first two weeks of school, to ease other students into having a transgender student on site. Over time, Star would begin using the girls' bathroom with a teacher standing outside of the door to make sure no one else would come in, for her protection. If needed, she could use one of four wheelchair bathrooms that could only be unlocked by a special education teacher or assistant. Unfortunately, the locations of those bathrooms turned out to be far away from her classes—as was the nurse's office.

Because Mr. Jones did not attend the meeting, he was not aware of anything that was agreed upon among the teachers. As Mr. Jones took attendance for the first day of school for the fifth-period gym class, he called out every name on the roster and asked the students to respond by saying, "Here!"

Mr. Jones: "Aster Davis."

Student: "Here!"

Mr. Jones: "Samuel Edmonds?"

There was a silence, and then the whispers began. Star had not heard this name in so long that she had forgotten that this was her "dead name." The name *Samuel* had not existed to her in her home for nine years; she had forgotten that this name was once associated with her.

Mr. Jones: "Samuel Edmonds?"

A student said, "There it is!" The student got up and started pointing.

The entire class broke out into laughter, and Mr. Jones laughed along with the class. Star could feel her face go from warm to steaming hot. She stood up angrily and said, "My name is Star Edmonds!"

Mr. Jones, "Well, thank you for clearing that up, son, but on this roster, you are Samuel, and that is what I am going by. And why are you in a dress? Go to the nurse's office and get this taken care of now. You are distracting my class!" Under his breath, Mr. Jones said, "Lord, pray for this child."

Star grabbed her items and took the hall pass from Mr. Jones to go to the nurse. Star was beyond angry and confused. She kept replaying the incident over and over in her head. She finally said to herself, "If he had just attended the meeting, this could have been avoided. I would not be going to the nurse's office on the first day of class." Star arrived at the front door of the nurse's office; if she turned left, she would walk into the office and have to explain the humiliating moment that had just occurred to her. If she kept walking straight, she would leave the building, walking out to freedom. Star walked out, then hid until school was dismissed.

At the end of the school day, the physical education teachers gathered for their department meeting to discuss the first impression of their classes. When it was Mr. Jones' turn, he shared the following with his colleagues:

Mr. Jones, "Team, I have a problem. There is a boy who dresses like a girl in my class. Did anyone get the memo on this Samuel Edmonds? On the first day of class, this Black boy just shows up to my class wearing a dress. What is happening to our Black family? I have never seen anything like this. I am just speechless. This is some devil's work. Did I miss something?"

The entire department was aware that Star (not Samuel) would be coming to class today and that Star was related to Benjamin Edmonds, the star soccer player of the school. All eyes moved to the department chair, Ms. Shelia Sanders. Mr. Jones was not in the mood to hear anything coming from Ms. Sanders. She was granted the department chair position instead of Mr. Jones three years ago, and he has been bitter about it ever since.

Ms. Sanders responded, "Victor, we all knew that Star was coming to your class. In fact, if you had attended the teacher conference last week, you would have known."

Mr. Jones said, "Shelia, what do you expect me to do with that? What happens if it has to go to the bathroom? What are we going to do about the bathrooms? There are too many questions here with no answers! How safe is it if that boy is around our girl students? Please don't tell me it is coming to the swim team because I can't handle this right now!"

Ms. Sanders, "Victor, first, let's begin with names. Your student's name is Star; Star uses the pronouns she, her, and hers."

Mr. Jones, "I do not care what pronouns it uses. You need to do something about that. This is not acceptable by God, and I am a God-fearing man. Staarrr's presence is distracting. Why is Stttaaarrrr even in my class? You put Stttaarrr in my class, didn't you?"

Ms. Sanders, "Victor! STOP! We all just got through our first day of school. Let's reconvene tomorrow. Your next class with Star is on Wednesday. Let's come up with a solution during tomorrow's meeting. Sounds good?"

Mr. Jones nodded and left the room. The other two teachers present, Mr. Washington and Mrs. Fields, left the room speechless. Ms. Sanders immediately called the principal and the assistant principal who oversaw physical education and set up a meeting.

At the Edmonds home, Debra and Star walked into the room talking about Star's first two classes. Star was doing her best not to talk about physical education. James and Benjamin walked in looking excited and exhausted, wanting to share their day. Now that everyone was home, the teenagers got twenty minutes to talk about what was great about their day, what was not so great, and what they were going to look forward to tomorrow. Being the youngest and the newest person to DuBois High, Star got a chance to go first.

Star shared, "What went great was that none of my teachers used my dead name." She continued, "What was not as great is that the bathrooms and the nurse's office are a bit far from my classes, so can we reevaluate this? I am looking forward to a new day!"

Star could not bring herself to share with her family how Mr. Jones and a student treated her during class today. She also could not tell them that she walked out of school during fifth period. She thought she was on the road to being a reckless teen. Maybe today was just a terrible day, and physical education on Wednesday would be better. Thank goodness for block scheduling, so there was time to recuperate from the mess of today.

## Bad Habits Die Hard

The days and weeks went by for Star with little improvement in her physical education class. It did not help that every time Mr. Jones saw her, he immediately handed Star a hall pass to go to the nurse, and like clockwork, Star would walk out of the building. It was the third week of school that Debra received a call at work from the school saying that Star had never attended her physical education class. Debra was confused because Star never mentioned not going to physical education, and it was unlike her not to attend class. After her call from the school, Debra called James on his cell. His last class of the day was a planning period, and he answered immediately.

Debra said, "James, Star has not been attending her physical education class. I just received a call from the school."

James, surprised, said, "What? I will call Ben before soccer practice and tell him to come home."

They hung up the phone, and Debra went over to the school to pick up Star. For someone who just skipped physical education, Star was rather chipper and talkative. Debra did her best not to throw off her mood, but she was deeply concerned. It was unlike Star to miss a class, especially physical education. When Debra and Star walked into the house, James and Ben were already standing in the living room.

Star laughed sarcastically, "What's going on?"

Debra responded, "I received a call from the attendance office today saying that you have not attended any of your physical education classes or swim practices. Star, tell us what is going on?"

Star yelled, "I don't want to talk about it!"

James replied, "Talk about what?"

Star started sobbing uncontrollably and fell into her mother's arms. After 30 minutes, Star was finally able to put words together that made sense.

Star said, breathing deeply between phrases, "Mr. Jones . . . and someone . . . called me an . . . "it" on the . . . first day of school. And . . . he . . . called . . . me . . . the name. . . . And he just . . . gives me . . . a pass to change . . . . clothes . . . at the nurse's office. Please don't be mad. I can't go to swim practice. I don't know what to do. I don't know what to do. This is my fault."

Debra and James looked at each other in shock. Ben felt guilty for not protecting his little sister. How could this happen to their child? Why did they not know? How could their child just walk out of school and never be questioned? How could their child not feel protected in a learning environment?

## Critical Race Study Discourse

1. What is your school district's policy on using a student's official name versus the name that the student and their family have recommended to use in a learning environment?

   a. Find and read the draft policy 8040 related to the Loudon County Public Schools found at: https://lcps.org/. Discuss how you would uphold this policy in your classroom.

2. How would you welcome a transgender student to your classroom? What guidelines would you provide without outing that specific student?

3. Identify gender-biased roles in your school. Why do you think they exist, and what do you think could change such roles in your school/education?

4. Identify all issues surrounding Star's use of the bathroom on school grounds. In your role, what would you do? What administrative policies would you challenge to make the use of bathrooms more inclusive? Provide a solution to your stated problem(s).

5. What are your thoughts about the bathroom plan devised during the meeting for Star?

6. How would you handle a student who became unruly while calling attendance? How would you have redirected the classroom?

7. What would you have said to Mr. Jones during the department meeting? Do you think it was appropriate for Ms. Sanders to state that Benjamin is Star's brother?

8. Does your school have a GSA? If so, would you participate? How would you participate? If not, discuss your reluctance.

9. If you saw or heard of a teacher like Mr. Jones in your school, what would you do? Would you act differently to him alone versus in front of your colleagues? How would you act?

10. What are the resources available to you to understand the LGBTQ+ community best?

## References and Suggested Resources

Anderson, Austin R., Eric Knee, William D. Ramos, and Tiffany Monique Quash. 2018. "'We Just Treat Everyone the Same': LGBTQ Aquatic Management Strategies, Barriers and Implementation." *International Journal of Aquatic Research and Education* 11 (1): 2. https://doi.org/10.25035/ijare.11.01.02.

Anderson, Eric, and Ann Travers, eds. 2017. *Transgender Athletes in Competitive Sport.* New York, Taylor & Francis.

Andrzejewski, Jack, Sanjana Pampati, Riley J. Steiner, Lorin Boyce, and Michelle M. Johns. 2020. "Perspectives of Transgender Youth on Parental Support: Qualitative Findings From the Resilience and Transgender Youth Study." *Health Education & Behavior* 48 (1): 74-81. https://doi.org/10.1177/1090198120965504.

Brockenbrough, Ed. 2016. "Becoming Queerly Responsive: Culturally Responsive Pedagogy for Black and Latino Urban Queer Youth." *Urban Education* 51 (2): 170-196. https://doi.org/10.1177/0042085914549261.

Case, Kim A., and S. Colton Meier. 2014. "Developing Allies to Transgender and Gender-Nonconforming Youth: Training for Counselors and Educators." *Journal of LGBT Youth* 11 (1): 62-82. https://doi.org/10.1080/19361653.2014.840764.

Daley, Andrea, Steven Solomon, Peter A. Newman, and Faye Mishna. 2007. "Traversing the Margins: Intersectionalities in the Bullying of Lesbian, Gay, Bisexual and Transgender Youth." *Journal of Gay & Lesbian Social Services* 19 (3-4): 9-29. https://doi.org/10.1080/10538720802161474.

Duncan, Garrett Albert. 2005. "Black Youth, Identity, and Ethics." *Educational Theory* 55 (1): 3-22. https://doi.org/10.1111/j.1741-5446.2005.0002a.x.

Human Rights Campaign. 2021. "HRC's Brief Guide to Getting Transgender Coverage Right," last updated June 2021. www.hrc.org/resources/reporting-about-transgender-people-read-this.

Loudon County Public Schools. 2021. Draft Policy 8040, Rights of Transgender and Gender-Expansive Students Code of Virginia §22.1-23.3, 8.01-217, 32.1-269(E). https://go.boarddocs.com/vsba/loudoun/Board.nsf/files/C35H9N449351/$file/Draft%20%20POLICY_%208040%20Rights%20of%20Transgender%20Students%205-6-21.pdf.

McCready, Lance T. 2004. "Understanding the Marginalization of Gay and Gender Non-Conforming Black Male Students." *Theory Into Practice* 43 (2): 136-143. www.jstor.org/stable/3701549.

National Center for Transgender Equality. 2016. "Frequently Asked Questions About Transgender People," last modified July 2016. https://transequality.org/issues/resources/frequently-asked-questions-about-transgender-people.

Simons, Jack D., Leeann Grant, and Jose M. Rodas. 2021. "Transgender People of Color: Experiences and Coping During the School-Age Years." *Journal of LGBTQ Issues in Counseling* 15 (1): 16-37. https://doi.org/10.1080/15538605.2021.1868380.

Singh, Anneliese A. 2013. "Transgender Youth of Color and Resilience: Negotiating Oppression and Finding Support." *Sex Roles* 68 (11): 690-702. https://doi.org/10.1007/s11199-012-0149-z.

Woodson, Ashley N., and Amber Pabon. 2016. "'I'm None of the Above': Exploring Themes of Heteropatriarchy in the Life Histories of Black Male Educators." *Equity & Excellence in Education* 49 (1): 57-71. https://doi.org/10.1080/10665684.2015.1121456.

Reed Kaestner/Corbis/Getty Images

# 8

# PETE Candidates Are Ill-Equipped to Teach Students in Black Urban Environments

*Cara Grant*

*PETE Standard 3. Planning and Implementation* (SHAPE America 2017)

Physical education candidates apply content and foundational knowledge to plan and implement developmentally appropriate learning experiences aligned with local, state, or SHAPE America's National Standards and Grade-Level Outcomes for K-12 Physical Education through the effective use of resources, accommodations and modifications, technology and metacognitive strategies to address the *diverse* needs of all students.

## Overview of Teacher Candidates

Mike, Danielle, John, and Andrea are four teacher candidates going through their internship this semester at KHMS. While they have experienced the same program, they come from different walks of life. Mike and Danielle went to high school together at the same urban school. Mike is a Black male who is a stellar athlete and avid gamer. He is the youngest in his family and a first-generation college student. Danielle is a biracial female, mixed Black and white. She often is perceived as white or Latina because of her fair-colored skin, but she sees herself as Black. John is a white male intern who grew up in a suburb of the urban school district's location. He has a diverse friend group in the cohort, but most of his classmates in high school and family members are white. Andrea is a white female student who grew up in a middle-class suburb near the urban district in a diverse high school with a population about 30 percent white, 30 percent Black, 30 percent Latino, and 10 percent Asian Pacific Islander.

Mike is a source of pride for his family, because he is the first person in his family to attend college. His family has experienced ups and downs. In his neighborhood, Mike was routinely profiled by police officers. Mike's parents—caring, hardworking, churchgoing people—provided life lessons on how to survive as a Black person, "You have to work ten times as hard as any white person to make something of yourself." Mike's dad has a high school diploma, and his mom took a few college courses, but they didn't further their own education because they needed to work to make ends meet and provide for the family. Mike used video gaming to "lay low," keep in the house, and stay out of trouble. Mike's passion for playing sports also kept him occupied, along with a teacher who believed in him beyond the scope of his neighborhood—a mentorship that helped Mike reach Physical Education Teachers College.

Danielle attended the same urban high school as Mike. Although she has light skin, her hair texture should inform people that she is Black. However, she constantly has to validate and prove who she is. For some, she is not dark enough; for others, she is not light enough. Sadly, instead of asking her name, people ask, "What are you?" Known as "lemon drop" after reading a Black history poem with that description, Danielle always battled people wanting to put her into a racial checkbox and force stereotypic expectations onto her. Like Mike's, her parents constantly worked, and she did extracurricular activities to keep her off the streets and to avoid negative influences.

In the nearby suburbs, John grew up unaware of his white male privilege and blind to the notion that his gender and skin color provided him advantages in the United States. His parents, both college-educated, gave John everything he needed, with the exception of summers, when he worked to pay for various expenses. John loved football and baseball and felt particularly close to his Black friends who were involved in the same activities.

Andrea lived in a different suburb, the same one where she had grown up and attended her neighborhood high school. A product of a blended house, school-aged Andrea traded weekends with her mom and dad, living with her mom during the week. She is still the key caregiver for her younger half-siblings, who came along after her mom remarried. This experience limited her ability to do a lot of extracurricular activities. Her high school had a diverse population of Black, white, Latinx, and Asian students. She has friends of different races.

At this moment, Mike, Danielle, John, and Andrea are starting their official internships and are excited about becoming physical education teachers. They receive the same placement, KHMS, where they have been working with a seasoned mentor teacher and are now preparing for teaching their first lesson. Mike is on locker room duty and uses this time to get to know students by asking them questions. In the same locker room, John is also trying to talk to students, but most do not acknowledge him. In the girls' locker room, Danielle and Andrea are learning to supervise and are engaged in chitchat with the students, discussing sports, college, and other interests like manga and anime. As students leave the locker room, the interns go in different directions to teach their lessons independently.

Mike is starting his lesson with an activity where students play a small game until everyone is out of the locker room. When all students are out of the locker room, he blows his whistle and meets with the week's "team captain." From there, Mike lets the captain know the expectations for the day. While the captain is listening to the expectations, the student athletic trainer is leading students through dynamic and static warm-ups. Some students are goofing around, but when the captain gathers them and shares the routine and expectations, they get back on task. When Mike blows the whistle again, students know that is a signal to come in and hear from the teacher, so they meander over to the portable whiteboard where Mike has written the objective, question for the day, and agenda. He goes through these items and sends the team back to their space. Throughout the lesson, Mike is rotating and monitoring play. He freezes certain aspects of the game to highlight defending space and other tactical game concepts that align with the objective. At the end of the lesson, he blows a whistle, and students come back to the whiteboard to listen again. He shares the closure for the lesson and then uses a practice called "all hands in," where everyone on the team puts their hand in a circle until each person has spoken. This is to emphasize elevating every voice on the team and holding everyone accountable.

The next group of students is in John's class. He uses a similar structure for learning as Mike does. As students come to the teaching space, he says hello and calls the students by name. Some names he does not remember or does not know how to pronounce, but he confidently says them as if he thinks he is correct. He is happy he can remember all the names, even if he is pronouncing them wrong. As students come, he does not trust the students to work independently, so when he blows the whistle, he uses his loud PE voice and warmly invites all the students to come in and sit in squad lines. Students are to listen and be quiet the whole time as John goes over the objective, agenda, and critical thinking question for the day. He keeps getting interrupted by a group of students and tells them to be quiet while praising a couple of white girls for paying attention. He says, "I wish everyone else could listen like you girls do." One of the boys yells at him, and he is scared because the boys are bigger than he is and they are Black. He is worried that they will attack him in the locker room or do something to his car. He doesn't know how to respond to these boys. He gives up and changes his expectations for the class. He lowers his expectations by changing the lesson to one where he is leading from an activity-based mindset. His focus is merely to try to keep them busy, happy, good, or compliant.

When asking questions, John only calls on students with their hands up or white students. When he is done with the whole group instruction, he sends students to their designated areas to begin dynamic and static warm-ups led by the athletic trainer. This doesn't work, so he yells, "Go ahead and play your game when you are ready." He doesn't trust a few students who have been known to be off task, so he stays close to them throughout the class. He tries to get to know them, but they just look at him like he doesn't get it. The class moves along, and then he blows the whistle and calls all students in for closure.

As John is closing out the class, he tries to embarrass the students who were off task during the class and blasts them in front of their peers. Instead, they ignore him, and someone else in the class yells, "Get a clue! You don't care. Why should they? You are just visiting. We live here."

In the indoor gymnasium, Danielle's students begin their lesson with a routine of walking and jogging around the teaching space until the whistle blows. When the whistle blows, students go to their designated team space. She is proud that things are going well, but even then, she sees some students are not in their teams. They are in other teams with their friends. She only realizes this after taking attendance, because she does not know all the students. Danielle feels like she hasn't connected with the students yet, so she tries something different: She checks in with each of the teams doing dynamic and static warm-ups, convenes a team meeting, and quickly shares with the teams that she also grew up in the same area they live in and is really excited to have her teaching internship there. Noticing students who are not with their true team, she reminds them of their team location. Sharing with the team captain the outline for the activities and small-sided games, she feels lucky to work with the students.

While Danielle is checking in with teams doing small-sided games, a verbal altercation begins. She runs over to see what is going on, stops play among the team having issues, and encourages the rest of the teams to continue what they are doing. She calls for a time-out and huddles with the team to investigate what is occurring. It turns out that someone made a wrong call about who should have possession of the ball, and it caused an argument. She asks the team, "What happens when we argue?"

A student says, "We get mad."

Danielle continues, "What else happens?"

A different student says, "We waste time and don't get to play."

"Exactly! It also takes a lot of fun out of the game and our class," says Danielle. "What can we do to resolve an argument quickly and restart play?"

One student replied, "We could talk about it."

Another student spoke up: "How about that game we played in elementary school—Rock, Paper, Scissors? We could do that, and the winner would get the call."

Danielle concludes, "That seems fair. Try that and let me know how that works and if we need to change it to resolve another conflict. Remember to communicate civilly when there is a disagreement in class. Thanks, everyone, for talking through the problem."

In the small teaching space, Andrea has students help set up the equipment while others are sitting and waiting. Once she is ready, she goes over the objective and asks students some questions. She randomly calls on students using a random-choice app on her phone, in hopes that it will get more students involved. The students know that she is not trying to catch them off guard. She really thinks it is important for every student to have a voice and for the students to know that she believes in them, because she knows they all have difficult times at home. She thinks that they do not have an active father in their lives, so she wants to make sure she can do what she can to help support them at school. Andrea really wants to earn the trust of the students, and that's why she asks them to help her set up the small gym. When she starts with the questions, students are sitting in squads. Half of the students look like they don't care, and the other half look bored.

Andrea tries to get them involved and asks what they know about the sport of lacrosse. She thinks that people who play this are mostly white; she chose this sport because she wants to teach them something they don't know. When she randomly calls on the first student, she asks, "What is the game of lacrosse?" The student does not respond. "Okay," Andrea said, trying to sound upbeat, "Anyone know?" She looks frazzled and moves on to the next question, "Okay! All right. Who knows about the history of lacrosse?" She received blank stares. Andrea says, "Okay. Well, since no one knows about this, I am going to tell you what I know about the sport of lacrosse to help you all learn about it." She spends five minutes talking about lacrosse, from history to how to hold a stick to how to play. Then she puts on a five-minute video clip where white male players demonstrate how to play the sport of lacrosse. She is proud of the fact that she uses technology to call students equitably, so she is not calling on one student all the time. Sometimes, teachers only call on the students who raise their hand first, but she selects them randomly by loading the class roster into an app and spinning a wheel to see who should respond to the question. She even used a video clip to show these kids how to play lacrosse. She is quite proud of her planning in the lesson even though none of the students responded to her introduction questions.

# Job Fair

At the university job fair, the student teachers learn that there are job openings in the Black Urban School District (BUSD) where they interned—practically guaranteeing a position—while the neighboring districts do not have any openings. The BUSD has high turnover. The four interns share some thoughts about their career and job application strategies and options. The students are nervous and excited about the idea of applying to schools. The internship really gave them a great opportunity to build their repertoire of teaching and confidence as new teachers in urban schools.

The interns' thoughts vary. Mike really wants to work in the Black Urban School District because he feels that students should have teachers that look like themselves. Danielle wants to work wherever she can get hired, but she is particularly interested in the Black Urban School District, because she values the relationships developed during the internship and grew up in the district. John is more hesitant than his peers but does not share why with the group. Internally, he is conflicted. While he wants to teach, he feels threatened by big Black male students in the district and doesn't feel as if he can connect or relate to their experiences. He would rather work in a different school district or at Home Depot until a teaching position opens in the whiter school districts. Andrea really wants to be the parent figure and help all the Black students but does not feel comfortable with the large class load. She tells her group that she is looking for a school in the suburbs with more diversity than the Black Urban School District but will stay with her parents in the meantime.

## Critical Race Study Discourse

1. What implication does the diversity standard cited at the beginning of the case study have for preparing students for teaching? What would a comprehensive approach with practical application of culturally relevant instructional practices look like, in your opinion? How could this experience be further enhanced?

2. How does the intersectionality of our circumstances grant us or deny us privilege? How does where we come from impact how we teach?

3. Identify some culturally responsive teaching that did and did not happen with Mike, Danielle, John, and Andrea's teaching. Why were these practices culturally responsive or not culturally responsive?

4. What are equitable practices in education? As a new preservice teacher or teacher in practice, how do you identify common ways to increase engagement in your classes through equitable practices?

5. What were the low expectations used by the PETE interns at the urban high school? How could they be modified to high expectations? What high expectations and practices were used to build trust and relationships in the classroom?

6. Research Title I schools, including the criteria and academic and social outcomes of these schools.

7. Define the white savior complex and give some examples. Where do you see the white savior complex in the case study? In schools? In research?

## References and Suggested Resources

Angelou, Maya. 1994. "The Complete Collected Poems of Maya Angelou." *Human Family*. New York: Random House.

Crenshaw, Kimberlé. 2022. *On Intersectionality: Essential Writings*. New York: The New Press.

Gay, Geneva. 2018. *Culturally Responsive Teaching: Theory, Research, and Practice*. 3rd ed. New York: Teachers College Press.

Hammond, Zaretta. 2015. *Culturally Responsive Teaching and the Brain*. Thousand Oaks, CA: Corwin Press.

Miller, Lisa A., and Victor W. Harris. 2018. "I Can't Be Racist—I Teach in an Urban School, and I'm a Nice White Lady!" *World Journal of Education* 8 (3): 1-11. https://files.eric.ed.gov/fulltext/EJ1182572.pdf.

SHAPE America. 2017. "National Standards for Initial Physical Education Teacher Education." https://www.shapeamerica.org/accreditation/upload/National-Standards-for-Initial-Physical-Education-Teacher-Education-2017.pdf.

# Conclusion

Diverse experiences manifest in physical education programs for Black youth. Common themes of dehumanization in teacher training and practice, however, collectively create narratives that stifle Black excellence in physical education spaces. On average, Black students have lower-quality physical education opportunities than their white counterparts. In a report on New York's physical education programming (considered one of the best), Black students receive less time allocated to physical education, do not have certified PE teachers, and have inadequate gymnasiums and outdoor spaces, especially during the primary years (Chapman 2017). Depriving students of the basic educational and fundamental movement needs sets an unstable foundation to engage in physical activity over the lifespan. Stolen youth and livelihood based on egregious, anti-Black, adult decision-making plants the seeds of disengagement. Somehow we expect miraculous outcomes while blaming students for failures. As the African proverb says, *It takes a village to raise a child*, and everyone who comes in contact with Black students must contribute to their success. To establish holistic, culturally responsive, and anti-racist physical education environments for Black students, we offer eight considerations to foster change.

### 1. Examine the impact of the hidden curriculum.

There is a hidden curriculum in every school and classroom that transmits unstated norms, values, and beliefs through the underlying educational structure (Culp 2014). Black students navigate through schools' "microsystems," which reflect a host of racist and dehumanizing behaviors (Bronfenbrenner 1979; Ross and Bondy 2013). Perspectives still suggest that the failure and misbehavior of youth are "business as usual" in today's schools (Howard 2008). This normalization of school policies and practices is seen in how students are assigned to classes, grouped, and disciplined. Black students are still tracked into educational opportunities that diminish their confidence and self-efficacy. They are overrepresented when discipline policies are enforced (e.g., zero-tolerance) and cited often for subjective behaviors such as "disrespect" and "excessive noise" (Ross and Bondy 2013). Implicit and explicit messages about Black youth are conveyed in discourses about improving schools, while at the same time, school districts and teachers avoid (or shun) conversations about race and structural inequality (Noguera 2008). This inaction has implications for policy and practice because it serves to perpetuate existing stereotypes of Black youth while reinforcing the notion that they are "less than"—whether it be "less smart, less capable, or less attractive" (Noguera 2008, p. 7).

2. **Question and address mechanisms of cultural reproductions in society and schools.**

To do so, we encourage faculty to implement early research and cultural field experiences that require PETE candidates to conduct comparative analyses of physical education programs across schools that vary in their racial composition, examining the disparities in programming, policy, and structures that are seen and unseen. And, because teachers tend to teach how they were taught and according to white cultural norms (Jester and Fickle 2013; Ladson-Billings 2006; VanDeusen 2019), teacher candidates should engage in cross-cultural field experiences early and often to adequately prepare teacher candidates to teach in diverse settings—a practice shown to be effective in PE and non-PE settings (Shiver, Richards, and Hemphill 2019). Cultural field experiences have helped white teacher candidates identify their biases and increase empathy for those from different cultural and racial identities (VanDeusen 2019).

3. **Engage in intentional teacher recruitment and mechanisms to identify and retain Black teachers.**

It is no secret that the teaching profession is not as racially diverse as it should be. Black women teachers occupy just 5 percent of the teaching workforce, while Black men make up less than 2 percent (USDOE 2016). As expressed earlier, Black youth benefit from the addition of Black teachers to schools. When supported, these teachers can inspire students and develop meaningful relationships that reduce feelings of alienation and neglect. Barriers that have contributed to a low number of Black teachers in schools involve cultural, economic, and systemic challenges. These include lack of support for Black preservice candidates in their preparation programs, the cost of initial teacher certification exams, higher rates of exam failure attributed to how they are designed, worry about future student debt, and the prevalence of low teaching salaries. Some methods by which to recruit teachers include preapprenticeships, incentivizing through scholarship or funding initiatives, and pipeline programs. However, even when Black teachers earn school positions, they often are subjected to "invisible taxes" that include increased scrutiny of their teaching methods, being overutilized as disciplinarians, and lack of collegial support. These and other adverse teaching conditions (e.g., racial discrimination, stereotyping, additional workloads) are contributing factors to the higher turnover among Black teachers than non-Black teachers after five years in the profession

(Carver-Thomas 2018). The future of Black youth success in physical education demands attention to proactive hiring practices, ongoing mentoring and support for Black teachers, and acknowledgment and action to eliminate teacher representation gaps.

4. **Include alternative qualitative assessments to determine teacher effectiveness.**

Current preservice assessment tools used to determine effective instruction employ a one-size-fits-all approach and fail to include student voices and culturally responsive strategies. Illustrating this practice is the Candidate PreService Assessment of Student Teaching (CPAST) instrument, widely used to evaluate student teachers using standards that do not consider complexities across schools, especially the geographical, social, economic, cultural, and racial demographics of students. Previous work illuminates that U.S. (physical) education standards are rooted in whiteness and can contain biases (Blackshear and Culp 2021; Spies 2004; Walton-Fisette and Sutherland 2020; Weilbacher 2012), and based on the "sameness" of CPAST, these biases are perpetuated. Furthermore, textbooks aligned to the standards also follow a pattern of no representation or ill-reporting of racially, culturally, or gender-diverse groups (Grant and Tate 1995; Simms 2013). Although CPAST includes "culture" and "culturally relevant" language in its rubrics, what this means in practice is open to interpretation for teacher-educators that have consistently shown a lack of cultural competencies themselves (Gay 2010; Ladson-Billings 2006; Simms 2013; Weilbacher 2012). To compensate for these deficiencies and better prepare teacher candidates to work in diverse schools, we suggest employing the racial equity standards in physical education teacher education (PETE) (see appendix A) as a starting point to establishing cultural responsiveness and racial awareness competencies among PETE candidates.

Simms (2013) recommends an "action research" approach, focusing on risk-taking and self-reflection when we are teaching the methods and designing the courses to develop a culturally conscious curriculum. However, teacher-educators have dismissed the power of the approach (Kemmis and McTaggart 2008), despite ample evidence that action research is a useful tool for preservice teachers to develop cultural consciousness (Martin 2005; Tormey and Henchy 2008). Simms conducted action research with teachers of various disciplines who were taking her curriculum planning course, using several risk-taking teaching methods (e.g., students reviewing curriculum and textbooks, interviewing content creators, and responding to reflective questions) rather than lecture. PETE candidates can employ the Physical Education Equity Policies and Practice (see appendix B) as a simplified action research practice activity in methods courses that use data (qualitative and quantitative) instead of physical education standards to critically examine, interrogate, and reflect on physical education policies, content, practices, and student identities to foster an equitable environment for all. Last, and to determine ongoing teacher impact on students, teacher candidates and practitioners should continually ask pupils in physical education qualitative questions regarding teaching behaviors throughout the year to help identify culturally responsive practices and practices that cause harm—the student-voice component missing from CPAST and other teacher evaluative tools.

5. **Understand the importance of imagery to make physical education meaningful for Black students.**

   Stereotypes of African Americans have been deeply ingrained in our society using imagery and tropes that have restricted perceptions of who Black youth can be. The images that are provided from the media through social construction establish white students as normative and superior while establishing Black people as inferior. As Sealey-Ruiz and Greene (2015) note, the historical characterization of Blacks depicts them as Toms, coons, mulattoes, mammies, and bucks. Black boys are interpreted as "savages" or "brutes," while girls have been framed as ill-mannered, hot-tempered, and highly sexualized. Even when the intent is meant to be positive, Black youth are often framed as physically superhuman, insightful beyond the scope deemed possible, overly optimistic, or an exception that makes people feel good. Ultimately, youth see what is interpreted, and when these associations begin to become unpacked in the classroom, there is an interaction that influences how one is perceived racially in the physical and social world (Van Ausdale and Feagin 2001).

   With this understood, teachers need to be intentional about how they design their spaces. In teaching materials (slides, worksheets, boards, posters), there should be care in selecting images that are not only of white people and photographs to foster connections. Clip art images or cartoons must be examined for unnecessary exaggerations or stereotypes of facial or bodily features. Choosing visual representations of Black people in normal roles that youth see on a routine basis (instead of just athletes and entertainers) humanizes Black existence and communicates that it is okay for Black people to simply be. With the acknowledgment that Black people are not a monolithic group, it may also be appropriate to have youth take part in creating imagery and visuals to be used in the class. This can take place by allowing students to provide pictures of their physical activity experiences or having them post, on a common wall, artifacts related to their lives.

**6. Create a culture that views the Black body as positive.**

Since the arrival of Africans on U.S. slave ships, the Black body has served as a machine to perform work for the prosperity of white people. From plantations to athletic fields, Black bodies are monetized and commoditized. Winning at the expense of Black bodies is most evident in the National Basketball Association (NBA) and the National Football League (NFL), where Black bodies do the physical work, while the predominantly white owners and coaches control the players and reap the biggest dividends (Eitzen 2016). In other traditionally white arenas, Black bodies have entered and shown success. Notably, Serena Williams, Simone Biles, and Misty Copeland have elevated tennis, gymnastics, and dance, respectively, despite attempts to diminish their accomplishments by regulating their bodies and performances through white concepts of femininity and movement rather than acknowledging the brilliance, expression, value, and beauty that the Black body brings to these spaces (Aquirre 2020; Love and Maxwell 2020; Rhodan 2016; Winter et al. 2019). Unfortunately, similar dehumanizing practices are evident in schools with the regulation of Black expressions, including clothing and hairstyles, which have deleterious effects on well-being.

In contrast to athletic performative bodies, obesity is negatively associated with Black girls and women while ignoring body mass index metrics and medical manipulation aligned to the white male body (Katch and McArdle 1983; Strings 2019). Furthermore, similarly high rates of obesity among white women (42.2%) compared to Black women (49.6%) (Centers for Disease Control and Prevention 2020) do not garner the same negative attention. Moreover, Black male athletic build ideals propagated through the media and college and professional sport are atypical in the average PE classroom (Harrison and Belcher 2006).

Physical education environments can foster positive images of the Black body by understanding that Black cultural norms of beauty do not align with thinness (Winter et al. 2019). Thus, the focus should be on the efficiency of movement and the benefits of physical activity. In addition, racial and gender representation and affirmations have a positive impact on children. Therefore, teachers should include diverse images of Black people in various activities, body shapes, and skin tones to celebrate differences in beauty within and across groups.

**7. Understand that students are spatial, and this has ramifications for Black youth.**

Proulx et al. (2016) reflect on the notion that human beings have always been spatial when addressing how they find themselves in the world. The world we live in is a space shaped by the activities we engage in and compels us to consider the interaction between the environment, body, and mind. Spatial interactions may provide definitions of who we are, our limits, and our relationships with other individuals. In the modern day, ideas abound on how environments can be configured to be practical, safe, efficient, and accessible (Marquardt 2011). This is no different for youth, who are presented with opportunities to learn in spaces through making connections outside of the physical education environment. The positioning of the Black body and lingering structural inequalities that continue to persist in our society have ramifications for how space is navigated for Black youth. Consequently, physical education teachers would benefit by incorporating a Black spatial imagination in their practices.

As Towne and Meyer (2017) note, a Black spatial imagination is an imagining of space where Blackness is not only permissible but also culturally transformational. It is a mode where the history of how Black bodies have been politically and economically placed is acknowledged. A Black spatial imagination allows for futuristic visions of how Black youth can define themselves in all forms, including movement. It provides an opportunity for anti-Blackness to be interrogated in schools toward a better society for Black people. Jenkins (2021) succinctly says the following:

> Terror is spatialized in bodies, buildings, minds, classrooms, and other physical locations around schools. It is experienced in the routinized policies, practices, arrangements, and structures that work in tandem to perform the labor of terror. . . . Consequently, the spatialized terror that Black youth experience is a permanent condition of schooling that is inseparable from their everyday realities. For Black people inhabiting school spaces, the everydayness of terror is lived in the witnessing of pain endured by their Black peers. The exhibitions of terror consist of forcing students to observe other Black bodies being forcibly removed from the classroom and school community; the constant rejection of Black language, traditions, music preferences, and other cultural forms of expression; the obliteration of Black names and by extension Black identities. (p. 120)

8. **Find spaces for Black excellence rather than support white villainy, white concepts of qualification, and white savior complexes.**

Oluo (2020) asserts that all people of color (and white women) have "been instructed to value and strive toward the white [heterosexual] male version of success" (13), leaving little space for others to excel. Replications of white versions of success that limit Black excellence are evident in the fabric of physical education—namely, the current initial PETE and K-12 PE standards that have no representations of Black people, thought, or language (Blackshear and Culp 2021; Walton-Fisette and Sutherland 2020), and the disparate physical education conditions in predominantly Black schools (Chapman 2017; Harrison and Belcher 2006). Hence, Black excellence occurs in spite of anti-Black structural systems.

Unfortunately, many forms of Black excellence do not qualify or quantify according to white parameters. Moreover, when Black excellence emerges, it is often discounted and not given adequate attention, especially when it transcends beyond athletics or defies the racial glass ceiling (Brooks 2017). While authentic allyship is desired and required to achieve racial equity and social justice, it should be noted that white villainy, white concepts of qualification, and white savior complexes are threats to Black excellence. Coming to the rescue of Black people perceived as incapable and incompetent is an aggressive form of villainy, because whiteness continues to be the version of success. Performative acts of allyship do not help. When Black children in PE spaces do not appear to thrive, or when they resist non-affirming curricula and practices, the environment (e.g., space, standards, curriculum, approaches) needs adjustment, not the Black students who are often blamed.

# Future Directions and Relevance for Other Groups

While we focus on the humanity of Black people in physical education, we value all groups, especially those confronted with obstacles based solely on arbitrary and socially constructed paradigms that work against democracy and human rights for all. When Black people have equal access to opportunities, all groups that are marginalized or othered benefit by extension. With this in mind, we challenge PETE students and faculty to use the Creating a Case Study (see Lesson Considerations) activity to examine the unique barriers that other racial, ethnic, gendered, marginalized, and minoritized groups experience to work toward equity, inclusion, and social justice to ensure "life, liberty, and the pursuit of happiness."

# References

Aquirre, Abby. 2020. "Simone Biles on Overcoming Abuse, the Postponed Olympics, and Training During a Pandemic." *Vogue*, July 9, 2020. www.vogue.com/article/simone-biles-cover-august-2020.

Blackshear, Tara B., and Brian Culp. 2021. "Transforming PETE's Initial Standards: Ensuring Social Justice for Black Students in Physical Education." *Quest* 73 (1): 22-44. https://doi.org/10.1080/00336297.2020.1838305.

Bronfenbrenner, Urie. 1979. *The Ecology of Human Development: Experiments by Nature and Design*. Cambridge, MA: Harvard University Press.

Brooks, Roy L. 2017. *The Racial Glass Ceiling: Subordination in American Law and Culture*. New Haven, CT: Yale University Press.

Carver-Thomas, Desiree. 2018. *Diversifying the Teaching Profession: How to Recruit and Retain Teachers of Color*. Palo Alto: Learning Policy Institute. https://learning-policyinstitute.org/product/diversifying-teaching-profession-report.

Centers for Disease Control and Prevention. 2020. "Prevalence of Obesity and Severe Obesity Among Adults: United States, 2017-2018." www.cdc.gov/nchs/products/databriefs/db360.htm.

Chapman, Ben. 2017. "Public School Physical Education Programs Are Failing Black, Hispanic and Disabled Students." *New York Daily News*, June 28, 2017. www.nydailynews.com/new-york/black-hispanic-disabled-students-don-phys-ed-article-1.3286130.

Culp, Brian. 2014. "Lost in Translation." In *Sociocultural Issues in Physical Education: Case Studies for Teachers*, edited by Sarah Bernard Flory, Amy Tischler, and Stephen Sanders, 89-100. Lanham, MD: Rowman and Littlefield.

Culp, Brian, and J. Rose Chepyator-Thomson. 2011. "Examining the Culturally Responsive Practices of Urban Primary Physical Educators." *Physical Educator* 68 (4): 234-253. https://eric.ed.gov/?id=EJ961836.

Eitzen, D. Stanley. 2016. *Fair and Foul: Beyond the Myths and Paradoxes of Sport*. Lanham, MD: Rowman & Littlefield.

Grant, Carl A., and William F. Tate. 1995. "Multicultural Education Through the Lens of the Multicultural Education Research Literature." In *Handbook of Research on Multicultural Education*, edited by James A. Banks and Cherry A. McGee Banks, 145-166. New York: Macmillan.

Harrison, Louis, and Don Belcher. 2006. "Race and Ethnicity in Physical Education." In *Handbook of Physical Education*, edited by David Kirk, Doune Macdonald, and Mary O'Sullivan, 740-751. London: Sage. https://doi.org/10.4135/9781848608009.n41

Howard, Tyrone C. 2008. "Who Really Cares? The Disenfranchisement of African American Males in PreK-12 Schools: A Critical Race Theory Perspective." *Teachers College Record* 110 (5): 954-985. https://psycnet.apa.org/record/2009-00716-001.

Jenkins, DeMarcus A. 2021. "Unspoken Grammar of Place: Anti-Blackness as a Spatial Imaginary in Education." *Journal of School Leadership* 31 (1-2): 107-126. https://doi.org/10.1177/1052684621992768.

Jester, Timothy E., and Letitia H. Fickel. 2013. "Cross-Cultural Field Experiences in Alaska Native Villages: Implications for Culturally Responsive Teacher Education." *The Teacher Educator* 48 (3): 185-200. https://doi.org/10.1080/08878730.2013.793762.

Kalina, Peter. 2020. "Performative Allyship." *Technium Social Sciences Journal* 11 (August): 478-481. https://doi.org/10.47577/tssj.v11i1.1518.

Kaplan, Carolyn Shemwell, Erica M. Brownstein, and Kristall J. Graham-Day. 2017. "One for All and All for One: Multi-University Collaboration to Meet Accreditation Requirements." *SAGE Open* 7 (1). https://doi.org/10.1177/2158244016687610.

Katch, Frank I., and W.D. McArdle. 1983. *Nutrition, Weight Control, and Exercise.* Philadelphia: Lea & Febiger.

Kemmis, Stephen, and Robin McTaggart. 2008. "Participatory Action Research: Communicative Action and the Public Sphere." In *Strategies of Qualitative Inquiry,* 3rd ed., edited by Norman K. Denzin and Yvonna S. Lincoln, 271-330. Thousand Oaks, CA: Sage.

Ladson-Billings, Gloria. 2006. "It's Not the Culture of Poverty, It's the Poverty of Culture: The Problem With Teacher Education." *Anthropology & Education Quarterly* 37 (2): 104-109. https://doi.org/10.1525/aeq.2006.37.2.104.

Love, Jessica, and Lindsey Conlin Maxwell. 2020. "Serena Williams: From Catsuit to Controversy." *International Journal of Sport Communication* 13 (1): 28-54. https://doi.org/10.1123/ijsc.2019-0111.

Marquardt, Gesine. 2011. "Wayfinding for People With Dementia: A Review of the Role of Architectural Design." *Herd* 4 (2): 75-90. https://doi.org/10.1177/193758671100400207.

Martin, Renee J. 2005. "An American Dilemma: Using Action Research to Frame Social Class as an Issue of Social Justice in Teacher Education Courses." *Teacher Education Quarterly* 32 (2): 5-22. www.jstor.org/stable/23478719.

National Institute for Health and Care Excellence. 2013. "BMI: Preventing Ill Health and Premature Death in Black, Asian and Other Minority Ethnic Groups Public Health Guideline" [PH46]. www.nice.org.uk/guidance/ph46.

Noguera, Pedro A. 2008. *The Trouble With Black Boys and Other Reflections on Race, Equity, and the Future of Public Education.* San Francisco: Jossey-Bass.

Oluo, Ijeoma. 2020. *Mediocre: The Dangerous Legacy of White Male America.* New York: Seal Press.

Proulx, Michael J., Orlin S. Todorov, Amanda Taylor Aiken, and Alexandra A. de Sousa. 2016. "Where Am I? Who Am I? The Relation Between Spatial Cognition, Social Cognition and Individual Differences in the Built Environment." *Frontiers in Psychology* 7: 64. https://doi.org/10.3389/fpsyg.2016.00064.

Rhodan, Maya. 2016. "Across Generations and Professions, a President and a Prima Ballerina Talk About Race, Beauty and Breaking Barriers. In Conversation: Misty Copeland and Barack Obama." *Time* 187 (11): 56-60. https://time.com/4254551/president-obama-misty-copeland-transcript/.

Ross, D.D., and Elizabeth Bondy. 2013. Learning and unlearning racism: Challenging the hidden curriculum of schooling. In *At close range: The curious case of Trayvon Martin* (pp. 79-88). University of Florida: Center for the Study of Race and Race Relations.

Sealey-Ruiz, Yolanda, and Perry Greene. 2015. "Popular Visual Images and the (Mis)Reading of Black Male Youth: A Case for Racial Literacy in Urban Preservice Teacher Education." *Teaching Education* 26 (1): 55-76. https://doi.org/10.1080/10476210.2014.997702.

Shiver, Victoria N., K. Andrew R. Richards, and Michael A. Hemphill. 2020. "Preservice Teachers' Learning to Implement Culturally Relevant Physical Education With the Teaching Personal and Social Responsibility Model." *Physical Education and Sport Pedagogy* 25 (3): 303-315. https://doi.org/10.1080/17408989.2020.1741537.

Simms, Muriel. 2013. "A Teacher-Educator Uses Action Research to Develop Culturally Conscious Curriculum Planners." *Democracy & Education* 21 (2): 1-10. https://democracyeducationjournal.org/cgi/viewcontent.cgi?article=1093&context=home.

Spies, Paul. 2004. "On the Front Line in Minnesota's Social Studies Wars." *Rethinking Schools* 19 (1): 21-24. https://rethinkingschools.org/articles/action-education-on-the-front-line-in-minnesotas-social-studies-war.

Stanley, Linda S. 1995. "Multicultural Questions, Action Research Answers." *Quest* 47: 19-33. https://doi.org/10.1080/00336297.1995.10484142.

*Strings, Sabrina. 2019. Fearing the Black Body: The Racial Origins of Fat Phobia. New York* University Press.

Tormey, Roland, and Deirdre Henchy. 2008. "Re-Imagining the Traditional Lecture: An Action Research Approach to Teaching Student Teachers to 'Do' Philosophy." *Teaching in Higher Education* 13 (3): 303-314. https://doi.org/10.1080/13562510802045337.

Towne, S., and A.S. Meyer. 2017. *This Is a Black Spatial Imaginary* [Photography and Print Making]. Exhibited at Paragon Gallery, Center for Art and Contemporary Culture. August 1-October 14, 2017.

U.S. Department of Education, Office of Planning, Evaluation and Policy Development, Policy and Program Studies Service. 2016. "The State of Racial Diversity in the Educator Workforce." www2.ed.gov/rschstat/eval/highered/racial-diversity/state-racial-diversity-workforce.pdf.

Van Ausdale, Debra, and Joe R. Feagin. 2001. *The First R: How Children Learn Race and Racism.* Lanham, MD: Rowman & Littlefield.

VanDeusen, Andrea J. 2019. "A Cultural Immersion Field Experience: Examining Preservice Music Teachers' Beliefs About Cultural Differences in the Music Classroom." *Journal of Music Teacher Education* 28 (3): 43-57. https://doi.org/10.1177/1057083718824729.

Walton-Fisette, Jennifer L., and Sue Sutherland. 2020. "Time to SHAPE Up: Developing Policies, Standards and Practices That Are Socially Just." *Physical Education and Sport Pedagogy* 25 (3): 274-287. https://doi.org/10.1080/17408989.2020.1741531.

Weilbacher, Gary. 2012. "Standardization and Whiteness: One and the Same? A Response to 'There Is No Culturally Responsive Teaching Spoken Here.'" *Democracy & Education* 20 (2), article 15. https://democracyeducationjournal.org/home/vol20/iss2/15.

Winter, Virginia Ramseyer, Laura King Danforth, Antoinette Landor, and Danielle Pevehouse-Pfeiffer. 2019. "Toward an Understanding of Racial and Ethnic Diversity in Body Image Among Women." *Social Work Research* 43 (2), 69-80. https://doi.org/10.1093/swr/svy033.

# Definitions

**Ally**
A person who uses their privilege to advocate on behalf of someone else who does not hold that same privilege (Davenport 2018).

**Anti-Black Racism**
Anti-Blackness is defined in two parts. Part one refers to a process that strips Blackness of value (dehumanizes) and systematically marginalizes Black people. This form of anti-Blackness is overt racism. Society also associates politically incorrect comments with the overt nature of anti-Black racism. Beneath this anti-Black racism is the covert structural and systemic racism that predetermines the socioeconomic status of Blacks in the United States and is held in place by anti-Black policies, institutions, and ideologies.

Part two of anti-Blackness is the blatant disregard for anti-Black institutions and policies. This disregard is the product of class, race, or gender privilege certain individuals experience due to anti-Black institutions and policies (Council for Democratizing Education 2021).

**Colorism**
A practice of discrimination by which those with lighter skin are treated more favorably than those with darker skin. This practice is a product of racism in the United States in that it upholds the white standards of beauty and benefits white people in the institutions of oppression (National Conference for Community and Justice 2021).

**Critical Race Theory**
In the field of education, racial inequality is prominent in the areas of access, opportunity, and outcomes. Critical race theory (CRT) is a framework that offers researchers, practitioners, and policy makers a race-conscious approach to understanding educational inequality and structural racism to find solutions that lead to greater justice. Placing race at the center of analysis, critical race theory scholars interrogate policies and practices taken for granted to uncover the overt and covert ways that racist ideologies, structures, and institutions create and maintain racial inequality.

CRT is a helpful tool for analyzing policy issues such as school funding, segregation, language policies, discipline policies, and testing and accountability policies. It is also helpful for critically examining the larger issues of epistemology and knowledge production reflected in curriculum and pedagogy (Oxford Research Encyclopedia 2021).

### Cultural Appropriation

Theft of cultural elements—including symbols, art, language, customs, etc.—for one's own use, commodification, or profit, often without understanding, acknowledgment, or respect for their value in the original culture. Results from the assumption of a dominant (i.e., white) culture's right to take other cultural elements (Colours of Resistance Archive 2021).

### Cultural Racism

Cultural racism refers to representations, messages, and stories conveying the idea that behaviors and values associated with white people or "whiteness" are automatically "better" or more "normal" than those associated with other racially defined groups. Cultural racism shows up in advertising, movies, history books, definitions of patriotism, and policies and laws. Cultural racism is also a powerful force in maintaining systems of internalized supremacy and internalized racism. It does that by influencing collective beliefs about what constitutes appropriate behavior, what is seen as beautiful, and the value placed on various forms of expression (RacialEquityTools.org 2020).

Cultural norms and values in the United States have explicitly or implicitly racialized ideals and assumptions (for example, what the color "nude" means, which facial features and body types are considered beautiful, and which child-rearing practices are considered appropriate).

### Implicit Bias

Also known as unconscious or hidden bias, implicit biases are negative associations that people unknowingly hold. They are expressed automatically, without conscious awareness. Many studies have indicated that implicit biases affect individuals' attitudes and actions, thus creating real-world implications, even though individuals may not even be aware that those biases exist within themselves. Notably, implicit biases have been shown to eclipse individuals' stated commitments to equality and fairness, thereby producing behavior that diverges from the explicit attitudes that many people profess (RacialEquityTools.org 2020).

### Institutional Racism

Institutional racism refers specifically to how institutional policies and practices create different outcomes for different racial groups. The institutional policies may never mention a racial group, but their effect creates advantages for whites and oppression and disadvantage for people from groups classified as people of color.

#### Examples

- Government policies that explicitly restricted the ability of people to get loans to buy or improve their homes in neighborhoods with high concentrations of African Americans (also known as "redlining").

- City sanitation department policies that concentrate trash transfer stations and other environmental hazards disproportionately in communities of color (Leiderman, Bivens, and Major 2005).

## Intersectionality
Revealing [one's] multiple identities can help clarify the ways in which a person can simultaneously experience privilege and oppression. For example, a Black woman in America does not experience gender inequalities in the same way as a white woman, nor racial oppression in the same way as that experienced by a Black man. Each race and gender intersection produces a qualitatively distinct life.

Per Kimberlé Crenshaw, the originator of the term: Intersectionality is simply a prism to see the interactive effects of various forms of discrimination and disempowerment. It looks at the way that racism, many times, interacts with patriarchy, heterosexism, classism, xenophobia—seeing that the overlapping vulnerabilities created by these systems create specific kinds of challenges (Intergroup Resources 2021).

## Microaggression
The everyday verbal, nonverbal, and environmental slights, snubs, or insults, whether intentional or unintentional, that communicate hostile, derogatory, or negative messages to target persons based solely upon their marginalized group membership (Sue 2010).

## Othered or Othering
The process whereby an individual or groups of people attribute negative characteristics to other individuals or groups of people that set them apart as representing that which is opposite to them (Rohleder 2014).

## Race
A social construct and a concept that signifies and symbolizes social conflicts and interests by referring to different types of human bodies (Omi and Winant 2015).

## Racism
The belief that race is the primary determinant of human traits and capacities and that racial differences produce an inherent superiority of a particular race (Omi and Winant 2015).

## Restorative Justice
A theory of justice that emphasizes repairing the harm caused by crime and conflict. It places decisions in the hands of those who have been most affected by wrongdoing and gives equal concern to the victim, the offender, and the surrounding community. Restorative responses are meant to repair harm, heal broken relationships, and address the underlying reasons for the offense. Restorative justice emphasizes individual and collective accountability. Crime and conflict generate opportunities to build community and increase grassroots power when restorative practices are employed (The Movement for Black Lives 2020).

### White Fragility

A state in which even a minimum amount of racial stress becomes intolerable for white people, triggering a range of defensive moves. These moves include the outward display of emotions such as anger, fear, and guilt, along with behaviors such as arguing, silence, and leaving the stress-inducing situation. These behaviors, in turn, function to reinstate white racial equilibrium (DiAngelo 2018).

### Whiteness and White Racialized Identity

Whiteness and white racialized identity refer to the way that white people, their customs, culture, and beliefs operate as the standard by which all other groups are compared. Whiteness is also at the core of understanding race in America. Whiteness and the normalization of white racial identity throughout America's history have created a culture where non-white persons are seen as inferior or abnormal.

This white-dominant culture also operates as a social mechanism that grants advantages to white people since they can navigate society both by feeling normal and being viewed as normal. Persons who identify as white rarely have to think about their racial identity because they live within a culture where whiteness has been normalized (National Museum of African American History and Culture 2021).

### White Privilege

In "White Privilege: Unpacking the Invisible Knapsack," scholar Peggy McIntosh writes, "White privilege is like an invisible weightless knapsack of special provisions, maps, passports, code books, visas, clothes, tools, and blank checks." (McIntosh 1988) White privilege refers to the unquestioned and unearned set of advantages, entitlements, benefits, and choices bestowed on people solely because they are white. Generally, white people who experience such privilege do so without being conscious of it.

White privilege can also be structural. Structural white privilege is a system of white domination that creates and maintains belief systems that make current racial advantages and disadvantages seem normal. The system includes powerful incentives for maintaining white privilege and powerful negative consequences for trying to interrupt white privilege or reduce its consequences in meaningful ways. The system includes internal and external manifestations at the individual, interpersonal, cultural, and institutional levels.

The accumulated and interrelated advantages and disadvantages of white privilege are reflected in racial and ethnic inequities in life expectancy and other health outcomes, income and wealth, and other effects through different access to opportunities and resources. Such differences are maintained in part by denying that these advantages and disadvantages exist at the structural, institutional, cultural, interpersonal, and individual levels and by refusing to redress them or eliminate the systems, policies, practices, cultural norms, and other behaviors and assumptions that maintain them (McIntosh 1988).

**White Supremacy**
The idea (ideology) that white people and the ideas, thoughts, beliefs, and actions of white people are superior to people of color and their ideas, thoughts, beliefs, and actions. While most people associate white supremacy with extremist groups like the Ku Klux Klan and the neo-Nazis, white supremacy is ever-present in our institutional and cultural assumptions that assign value, morality, goodness, and humanity to the white group while casting people and communities of color as worthless (worth less), immoral, bad, inhuman, and undeserving. Drawing from critical race theory, the term "white supremacy" also refers to a political or socio-economic system where white people enjoy structural advantage and rights that other racial and ethnic groups do not, both at a collective and an individual level (RacialEquityTools.org 2021).

# References

"Anti-Black Racism." The Movement for Black Lives. Accessed August 1, 2021. http://web.archive.org/web/20200109004008/https:/policy.m4bl.org/glossary.

Bivens, Donna, Barbara Major, Maggie Potapchuk, and Sally Leiderman. 2005. *Flipping the Script: White Privilege and Community Building*. Center for Assessment and Policy Development, January 2005.

"Colorism." National Conference for Community and Justice. Accessed August 8, 2021. http://web.archive.org/web/20200109004008/https:/policy.m4bl.org/glossary.

"Cultural Appropriation." Colours of Resistance Archive. Accessed May 13, 2021. www.coloursofresistance.org/definitions/cultural-appropriation.

"Cultural Racism." The Movement for Black Lives. Accessed August 6, 2021. http://web.archive.org/web/20200109004008/https:/policy.m4bl.org/glossary.

Davenport, Lona. "Ally is Not a Noun." Accessed May 22, 2018. https://info.umkc.edu/diversity/ally-is-not-a-noun.

DiAngelo, Robin J. 2018. *White Fragility: Why It's So Hard for White People to Talk About Racism*. Boston: Beacon Press.

"Implicit Bias." The Movement for Black Lives. Accessed August 18, 2021. http://web.archive.org/web/20200109004008/https:/policy.m4bl.org/glossary.

"Intersectionality" Intergroup Resources. Accessed August 3, 2021. www.intergroupresources.com/intersectionality.

McIntosh, Peggy. 1988. White privilege and male privilege: A personal account of coming to see correspondences through work in women's studies. Working paper No. 189. Wellesley, Massachusetts: Wellesley Center for Research on Women.

Omi, Michael, and Howard Winant. 2015. *Racial Formation in the United States*. New York: Routledge.

Sulé, V. Thandi. "Critical Race Theory." *Encyclopedia of Social Work*, April 30, 2020. Accessed October 5, 2021. https://oxfordre.com/socialwork/view/10.1093/acrefore/9780199975839.001.0001/acrefore-9780199975839-e-1329.

"Restorative Justice." The Movement for Black Lives. Accessed August 1, 2021. http://web.archive.org/web/20200109004008/https:/policy.m4bl.org/glossary.

Rohleder, Poul. (2014) "Othering." In *Encyclopedia of Critical Psychology*, edited by T. Teo. New York: Springer.

Sue, Derald Wing . 2010. "Microaggressions: More than Just Race" *Psychology Today*, November 17, 2010.

"Whiteness and White Racialized Identity" National Museum of African American History and Culture: Talking About Race. Accessed August 3, 2021. https://nmaahc.si.edu/learn/talking-about-race/topics/whiteness.

"White Privilege." Racial Equity Tools. Accessed August 18, 2021. www.racialequitytools.org/glossary.

# Lesson Considerations

Students should create critical case studies based on the following scenarios to generate dialogue and debate, identifying the related systemic issues and teaching behaviors (including the long-term impact), while providing advocacy and activism strategies for change.

- Black male students are allowed to play basketball in PE every day, while Black female and nonbinary students are allowed to sit out.
- The PE teacher mispronounces a student's "ethnic" name even after the student has corrected the teacher several times. The teacher starts to use a nickname that the student hates.
- White students are the minority at this city school. The teacher notices that only the white students serve as leaders (as captains in PE and on athletic teams and leaders in school government). Black students are not represented in leadership roles.
- Black male high school student failing PE asks a Black woman teacher to "hook him up" because they share a racial identity.
- Faculty member does not want to submit a letter of recommendation for student teacher they believe is racist and will do more harm than good.
- Black students are treated favorably in physical education—assumed athletically inclined—whereas several teachers do not enjoy teaching the Asian and white kids because they view them as nonathletic.

## Creating a Case Study

Case studies are used as a means of applying ideas, theories, or concepts to a real situation. Case studies allow educators to check their biases while investigating sociocultural contexts that could impede the development and maintenance of equitable learning environments for all students (Gorski and Pothini 2018). In this book, we use case studies to help physical educators discuss issues that Black youth face in schools. Invariably, there will be situations that arise that are specific to a professional's situation. However, the process that we outline here for designing a case study can spur conversation, deeper learning, reflection, and strategic planning for change. For training purposes, specify parameters of how this assignment can vary based on needs.

Assignment: Create a case study that deals with a current issue affecting Black youth in your community that could be a barrier to effective physical education.

1. *Describe the problem or issue at hand.* This could involve asking a question, providing a brief statement, or developing a short narrative of an incident.

2. *Give background context.* What key facts and relevant information should be considered? Books, news, social media, and interviews (depending on time) are examples of resources that help to build context.

3. *Outline why this issue is important.* Create an outline of three or four main points that describe why it is necessary to address this issue. These can be supported by theory or best practices.

4. *Provide a solution.* Initially, solution(s) should be evenly balanced, with advantages and disadvantages.

5. *Hypothesize alternate solutions and conclusions.* As situations are ever-changing, it is appropriate to consider a range of perspectives and trends that could impact how we view current challenges.

# Reference

Gorski, P.C., and S.G. Pothini. 2018. *Case Studies on Diversity and Social Justice Education.* 2nd ed. New York: Routledge.

# Selected Resource List

## Articles in Physical Education

Blackshear, Tara B. 2020. "#SHAPEsoWhite." *Physical Education and Sport Pedagogy* 25 (3): 240-258. https://doi.org/10.1080/17408989.2020.1741533.

Blackshear, Tara B. 2021. "#SayHerName: Black Women Physical Education Teachers of the Year." *Journal of Teaching in Physical Education*. https://doi.org/10.1123/jtpe.2020-0308

Burden, Joe W., Samuel R. Hodge, Camille P. O'Bryant, and Louis Harrison Jr. 2004. "From Colorblindness to Intercultural Sensitivity: Infusing Diversity Training in PETE Programs." *Quest* 56 (2): 173-189. https://doi.org/10.1080/00336297.2004.10491821.

Clark, Langston. 2020. "Toward a Critical Race Pedagogy of Physical Education." *Physical Education and Sport Pedagogy* 25 (4): 439-450. https://doi.org/10.1080/17408989.2020.1720633.

Culp, Brian. 2020. "Physical Education and Anti-Blackness." *Journal of Physical Education, Recreation & Dance* 91 (9): 3-5. https://doi.org/10.1080/07303084.2020.1811618.

Culp, Brian. 2021. "Everyone Matters: Eliminating Dehumanizing Practices in Physical Education." *Journal of Physical Education, Recreation & Dance*, 92 (1): 19-26. https://doi.org/10.1080/07303084.2020.1838362.

Culp, Brian, and Martha James-Hassan. 2015. "Towards a Critical Discourse on the Black Experience in Canada and the United States: Implications for Physical Education." In *Social Justice in Physical Education: Critical Reflections and Pedagogies for Change*. Edited by Daniel B. Robinson and Lymm Randall, 63-82. Toronto, ON: Canadian Scholars Press.

Flintoff, Anne, and Fiona Dowling. 2018. "'I Just Treat Them All the Same, Really': Teachers, Whiteness and (Anti) Racism in Physical Education." *Sport, Education and Society* 24 (2): 121-133. https://doi.org/10.1080/13573322.2017.1332583.

Harrison, Jr., Louis, and Langston Clark. 2016. "Contemporary Issues of Social Justice: A Focus on Race and Physical Education in the United States." *Research Quarterly for Exercise and Sport* 87 (3): 230-241. https://doi.org/10.1080/02701367.2016.1199166.

Hylton, Kevin. 2015. "'Race' talk! Tensions and Contradictions in Sport and PE." *Physical Education and Sport Pedagogy* 20 (5): 503-516. https://doi.org/10.1080/17408989.2015.1043253.

Landi, Dillon, Tara B. Blackshear, and Carrie McFadden. 2021. "SHAPE America and Physical Literacy: An Event Horizon?" *Curriculum Studies in Health and Physical Education* 12 (2): 106-122. https://doi.org/10.1080/25742981.2021.1908835.

Simon, Mara. 2020. "The Emotionality of Whiteness in Physical Education Teacher Education." *Quest* 72 (2): 167-184. https://doi.org/10.1080/00336297.2020.1739541.

Thomas, Daniel J. III, Marcus W. Johnson, Langston Clark, and Louis Harrison Jr. 2020. "When the Mirage Fades: Black Boys Encountering Antiblackness in a Predominantly White Catholic High School." *Race Ethnicity and Education.* https://doi.org/10.1080/13613324.2020.1798376.

Walton-Fisette, Jennifer L., and Sue Sutherland. 2020. "Time to SHAPE Up: Developing Policies, Standards and Practices That Are Socially Just." *Physical Education and Sport Pedagogy* 25 (3): 274-287. https://doi.org/10.1080/17408989.2020.1741531.

## Organizations on Social Media

- Antiracism Center: Twitter
- Audre Lorde Project: Twitter | Instagram | Facebook
- Color of Change: Twitter | Instagram | Facebook
- Equal Justice Initiative (EJI): Twitter | Instagram | Facebook
- The Movement for Black Lives (M4BL): Twitter | Instagram | Facebook
- Showing Up for Racial Justice (SURJ): Twitter | Instagram | Facebook

## Guides

Smithsonian National Museum of African American History and Culture. "Talking About Race: Being Antiracist." https://nmaahc.si.edu/learn/talking-about-race/topics/being-antiracist

## Books

Abu-Jamal, Mumia. 2017. *Have Black Lives Ever Mattered?* San Francisco: City Lights Books.

Anderson, Carol. 2017. *White Rage: The Unspoken Truth of Our Racial Divide.* New York: Bloomsbury Adult.

Alexander, Michelle. 2012. *The New Jim Crow: Mass Incarceration in the Age of Colorblindness.* New York: The New Press.

Baldwin, James. 1992. *The Fire Next Time.* New York: Vintage.

Burke, Tarana, and Brené Brown, eds. 2021. *You Are Your Best Thing: Vulnerability, Shame Resilience, and the Black Experience—An Anthology.* New York: Random House.

Chugh, Dolly. 2018. *The Person You Mean to Be: How Good People Fight Bias.* New York: HarperCollins.

Coates, Ta-Nehisi. 2015. *Between the World and Me.* New York: Spiegel & Grau.

Cooper, Brittney. 2018. Eloquent Rage: A Black Feminist Discovers Her Superpower. New York: St. Martin's Press.

Du Bois, W.E.B. 2020. *The Souls of Black Folk.* New York: Penguin.

Fanon, Frantz. 2008. *Black Skin, White Masks.* New York: Grove Press.

Kendi, Ibram X. 2019. *How to Be an Antiracist*. New York: One World.

Kunjufu, Jawanza. 2012. There Is Nothing Wrong With Black Students. Chicago: African American Images.

Morrison, Toni. 2007. *The Bluest Eye*. New York: Vintage.

Oluo, Ijeoma. 2018. *So You Want to Talk About Race*. New York: Seal Press.

Oluo, Ijeoma. 2020. *Mediocre: The Dangerous Legacy of White Male America*. New York: Seal Press.

Yancy, George. 2008. *Black Bodies, White Gazes: The Continuing Significance of Race in America*. New York: Rowman & Littlefield.

## Other

- Soul 2 Soul Sisters: Ending Anti-Black Racism Resources: Twitter | Instagram | Facebook
- Learning for Justice: Twitter | Instagram | Facebook
- Jim Crow Museum: https://ferris.edu/HTMLS/news/jimcrow
- PhysEquity: https://physequity.wordpress.com/
- Support Real Teachers: Twitter | Facebook

# Appendix A

## *Racial Equity Standards in Physical Education Teacher Education*

*Standard 1: Describe the effects of enslavement, Jim Crow, and systemic racism.*

Candidates will...

1a. Discuss the enslavement of African people in America.

1b. Discuss the history of Jim Crow and segregation.

1c. Acknowledge through analysis that systemic racism is inherent throughout U.S. educational systems.

1d. Describe the negative outcomes that result from systemic racism on Black students.

1e. Identify causes of trauma and examine Black mental health; Discuss Post-Traumatic Slave Syndrome.

1f. Discuss the history of Black bodies performing physical work on plantations and on athletic fields.

1g. Draw analogies between enslavement and professional athletics (e.g., football, basketball).

1h. Discuss the exclusionary practices of Black people from physical education organizations.

1i. Describe the conditions of Black people pre- and post-integration – schooling, physical education, economics, housing.

*Standard 2: Discuss Black femininity and Black masculinity.*

Candidates will...

2a. Evaluate Black femininity and the Angry Black Woman label; evaluate Black masculinity and machismo persona.

2b. Evaluate sexuality (LGBTQ) and the concept of the Down Low in Black America.

2c. Discuss intimate and familial relationships (marriages, single-, two-parent, and multi-generational households) in Black communities.

*Standard 3: Demonstrate care, respect, and advocacy.*

Candidates will...

3a. Engage in anti-racist behaviors.

3b. Celebrate Black history and accomplishments yearlong.

3c. Identify and evaluate implicit and explicit biases.

3d. Monitor biases.

3e. Track and compare punishment and discipline data among all groups and genders.

3f. Engage in the direct recruitment of Black students into PETE programs.

3g. Describe effective advocacy strategies to promote physical education and physical activity opportunities for Black children.

3h. Support policies and laws that positively impact Black children.

3i. Request items/money from leadership; or, write a grant and develop other fundraising strategies to ensure all students have learning essentials.

3j. Volunteer in spaces with Black children.

*Standard 4: Demonstrate high expectations.*

Candidates will...

4a. Identify and focus on students' strengths.

4b. Inform students and parents of high expectations.

4c. Discuss the school-to-prison pipeline phenomenon.

4d. Identify how schools/teachers reproduce conditions that favor prison over education (e.g., excessive punishment of Black children).

4e. Analyze the causes of violence, incarceration, and the unfair sentencing of Black people.

4f. Hold students accountable for behaviors, work, and rule violations.

4g. Model expected behaviors.

4h. Assess students learning and provide immediate feedback.

*Standard 5: Demonstrate culturally consistent communicative competencies.*

Candidates will...

5a. Engage in cross-cultural/racial dialogue.

5b. Use direct, verbal communication.

5c. Collect language data and implement terminologies/language commonly used in Black communities.

5d. Demonstrate verbal and non-verbal affirmations of Black children.

5e. Affirm students with dark skin and natural Black hair.

5f. Implement literacy strategies shown effective for Black children (oral/verbal communication).

5g. Call or e-mail parents weekly with positive news about students.

### Standard 6: Content knowledge and application.

Candidates will...

6a. Describe content knowledge for teaching PK-12 physical education that includes Black people (athletes and non-athletes).

6b. Apply content knowledge for teaching PK-12 physical education that includes Black people.

6c. Incorporate and expose students to Black authors (fiction, nonfiction, textbooks, journal articles).

6d. Discuss the contributions of Black pioneers in physical education.

6e. Plan and implement learning experiences for students who do not have technology available of the same quality as those with.

6f. Invite Black scholars/teachers/parents to co-teach or lead a workshop.

### Standard 7: Implement skill- and fitness-building strategies.

Candidates will...

7a. Identify opportunities for students to engage in physical activity in the community (parks, home, school, gyms).

7b. Evaluate racial differences in motor skill development.

7c. Discuss and evaluate the Black athlete/Black sport vs. white athlete/white sport (myths vs. reality).

7d. Explore opportunities, or the lack thereof, that underpin physical activity and athletic outcomes/participation for Black, white, and other groups.

7e. Discuss racial and cultural differences in approaches to health-related fitness (e.g., body size/body composition, beauty norms, cultural expectations) and appreciate these differences.

7f. Discuss colorism and the impact on Black students' physical activity practices/behaviors (e.g., exercise outside in the sun).

7g. Evaluate the impact that racism has on health and fitness (e.g., stress response, cortisol release).

7h. Discuss why the white male body is the standard used for BMI measures and other anthropometric measures.

*Standard 8: Implement holistic instructional strategies.*

Candidates will…

8a. Encourage and allow students to express their individualism.

8b. Ask students (and parents of young children) the preferred ways of learning.

8c. Display representations of Blackness beyond sports where Black athletes are overrepresented (e.g., basketball and football).

8d. Examine and remove content knowledge that poses harm to Black students (e.g., stereotypes, deficit language).

8e. Adjust lessons/activities to meet students' needs.

8f. Describe and apply common content knowledge for teaching PK-12 physical education that includes Black people across all activities.

8g. Implement Black pedagogical strategies that promote a positive, safe, and engaging learning environment (e.g., African Pedagogical Excellence; African-Centered; Culturally Relevant/Sustaining; Abolitionist Education).

8h. Attend workshops and professional development that promote cultural awareness among Black children and their families.

Adapted by permission from T.B. Blackshear and B. Culp, "Transforming PETE's Initial Standards: Ensuring Social Justice for Black Students in Physical Education," *Quest* 73, no. 1 (2021): 22-44.

# Appendix B
## *PEEPP Analysis©*

## Physical Education Equity Policies and Practice (PEEPP) $=\dfrac{\text{Data}}{\text{Standards}}$

PEEPP Analysis is a tool that uses data instead of physical education standards to critically examine, interrogate, and reflect on physical education policies, content, practices, and the impact of practitioner and student identities to foster an equitable environment for all.

The following essential questions guide a racial PEEPP Analysis:

1. Where is racial equity evident in physical education?
2. How do we establish racial equity in physical education?

Mapping student and instructor identities and focusing on student needs are the first steps of the PEEPP Analysis. To illustrate the importance of how identity mapping affects the needs of students, in a recent survey regarding parental health concerns for children (Mott 2020), Black parents ranked racism and COVID-19 as the top two on their list of top 10 health concerns for their children. In contrast, the top two health concerns among white and Hispanic parents were the overuse of social media and bullying. Furthermore, racism and COVID-19 did not appear on the top 10 list of concerns among white parents but were numbers six and eight among Hispanic families. Furthermore, physical activity was absent from Black and Hispanic parents' top 10 list, while the lack of physical activity made the top five list among white parents. When combining parent data across all racial and ethnic groups, physical activity ranked number six, and COVID-19 ranked number 10. Racism did not make the top 10 list of health concerns, illustrating that louder or more voices have more choices as they drive the narratives for all.

Who are my students, and what do they need?

Who am I, and what impact does my identity have on students? (See figure B.1)

The more identity overlaps between the instructor and students, the easier it will be to engage in culturally responsive equitable approaches (see figure B.2). Conversely, the more distance or disconnect between instructor and student identities, the more challenging it will be to engage in culturally responsive equitable approaches.

The next steps are examining the remaining questions, finding solutions, and implementing strategies with continued reflection and examination (see figure B.3).

## Identity Mapping

**Who are my students?**

Race
Ethnicity
Social economics
Class
Culture
Political
Ability
Nationality
Sexuality
Gender
Education
Religion
Age
Mother tongue
Languages spoken
Language use

**Who am I?**

**Figure B.1**  Mapping student and instructor identities.

*Note:* Additional identities can be added.

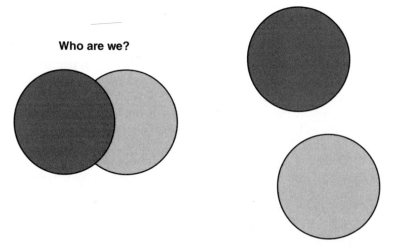

**Who are we?**

**Figure B.2**  Who are we together: Combining instructor and student identities.

# PEEPP Analysis©

## Policies

Who sets the standards?

What content are in the standards?

Who sets the curriculum?

Why are the standards and curriculum important?

How do the standards reflect equity?

How do the standards reproduce inequities?

## Practice

Who are my students?

Who am I?

What do my students need?

How do I engage with students?

How are my lessons liberating?

How are my lessons oppressive?

How can I achieve equity in PE?

**Figure B.3**   Physical Education Equity in Policy and Practice analysis.

© Tara B. Blackshear

# Reference

"Top Health Concerns for Kids in 2020 During the Pandemic." National Poll on Children's Health. Accessed January 6, 2021. https://mottpoll.org/reports/top-health-concerns-kids-2020-during-pandemic.

# About the Authors

Courtesy of Roy Cox Photography.

**Tara B. Blackshear** is an equity scholar who specializes in health, physical activity, and education. She is an assistant professor of kinesiology and the coordinator of the physical education teacher education program at Towson University. Before her current role, Dr. Blackshear taught for 17 years in public, private, charter, and international schools in the United States, Egypt, and Thailand. At the University of North Carolina at Chapel Hill, she held a three-year post in which she worked to prevent type II diabetes among middle school youth in the most extensive school-based physical activity intervention in the United States.

Dr. Blackshear's commitment to equity is evident in her work that appears in *Quest, Physical Education and Sport Pedagogy, Journal of Racial and Ethnic Health Disparities,* and numerous other journals. She is actively engaged with SHAPE America, SHAPE Maryland, Partnership for a Healthier America, Physical and Health Education Canada, International Association for Physical Education in Higher Education (AIESEP), USA Lacrosse, PhysEquity, and Baltimore City Public Schools.

Dr. Blackshear's research has garnered national and international attention. She has begun to have an impact on institutional change, policy, and practice, as evidenced by consultation requests from organizations and agencies that seek her help in their goal of creating culturally responsive, equitable environments. Dr. Blackshear's candid perspective has shown effectiveness in transforming institutions' performative gestures into measurable outcomes with accountability. *Critical Race Studies in Physical Education* furthers Dr. Blackshear's unwavering commitment to confront and disrupt structures that do not serve Black youth in health, physical activity, and education.

Courtesy of Kennesaw State University.

**Brian Culp** is a professor and department chair in the WellStar College of Health and Human Services at Kennesaw State University. Prior to his current position, Dr. Culp taught at Armstrong Atlantic State University and Indiana University–Purdue University Indianapolis.

Dr. Culp's research has incorporated topics under the umbrella of promoting equity. His work has appeared in journals such as *Quest, Pedagogy in Health Promotion, Qualitative Health Research, and International Journal of Sports Science & Coaching* as well as many other journals and books. He has also worked on projects for organizations such as Physical and Health Education Canada, SHAPE America, the Centers for Disease Control, and the National Board for Professional Teaching Standards.

Dr. Culp was inducted as the 34th fellow of the National Association for Kinesiology in Higher Education (NAKHE) in 2019—at the time, the youngest person to be awarded that distinction. He is a past vice president and Engaged Scholar Mentor of NAKHE. In recent years, Dr. Culp has been honored as a Delphine Hanna Lecturer (2017) and Dudley Allen Sargent Lecturer (2020). Other national recognitions have included a dissertation award from the Georgia Association of Teacher Educators; the Hally Beth Poindexter Young Scholar Award from NAKHE; and the Mabel Lee Award, the Social Justice and Diversity Young Professionals Award, and the E.B. Henderson Award from SHAPE America. Internationally, Dr. Culp has been a Fulbright-Hays program participant in Kenya and a Fulbright scholar and visiting research chair in Montreal. He currently serves as a Fulbright specialist.

# About the Contributors

**Angela K. Beale-Tawfeeq** is an associate professor and program coordinator of the health and physical education teacher education program in the department of science, technology, education, arts, mathematics, and movement education at Rowan University. Dr. Beale-Tawfeeq earned her BA in English, MS in therapeutic recreation from Howard University, MPH in community health at Arcadia University, and PhD in physical education teacher education from Florida State University. Dr. Beale-Tawfeeq's interest in addressing health disparities in the African American community and promoting equity and social justice via water safety and drowning prevention redirected her professional focus toward the inclusion of public health. Dr. Beale-Tawfeeq founded End Needless Drowning—an aquatic physical activity–based youth development program in underserved communities. Her research and academic pursuits include water safety and drowning prevention, community health, culturally competent physical activity program evaluation, and culturally responsive pedagogy in K-12 health and physical education. Dr. Beale-Tawfeeq is an advocate for programs and policies that aim to improve African American and Latino health.

**Afi C. Blackshear** earned his BA in political science from the University of California San Diego. After a brief stint in government relations in Washington, D.C., he returned to California to attend Stanford Law School. Since starting law school, Afi has become increasingly involved in the policy and legal matters that revolve around technology. Noting a lack of diversity in the field—particularly among the leadership ranks—Afi has become involved in increasing diversity in the tech industry. He is currently a Wetmore Fellow at the law firm Morrison & Foerster, and he is the creator of the podcast *The Periphery*.

Courtesy of Aaron Brumbelow.

**Akinyemi K. Blackshear** (he/they), currently residing in Savannah, Georgia, identifies as a queer Black male from the South. With a passion for the arts, Akinyemi aspires to remove barriers within the arts so all communities can access its transformative power. This aspiration developed after completing his BFA in dance at the University of North Carolina at Greensboro in 2017, when Akinyemi joined the Jacob's Pillow Dance Festival team as an intern. The internship combined his love for dance with his newly sparked passion for marketing, accessibility, and community engagement. Akinyemi eventually transitioned into other marketing roles at Jacob's Pillow, and in 2019 began working at the Savannah Music Festival to apply his knowledge in marketing to a different field within the arts. Akinyemi has served as part of the diversity, inclusion, equity, and accessibility (DIEA) task force at Jacob's Pillow and co-led Savannah Music Festival's DIEA task force. Currently, Akinyemi continues his work in the arts at Jacob's Pillow, focusing on digital marketing. He hopes to continue to create opportunities to develop his artistic dance work.

**Cara Grant** is the preK-12 health and physical education supervisor in a large Maryland school district. She is also a lecturer in the department of kinesiology and is the master of education with certification professional development schools coordinator with the College of Education at the University of Maryland College Park. Dr. Grant earned her undergraduate degree from the University of Maryland, master's degree from Bowie State University in secondary education with a specialization in curriculum and instruction, and doctorate in education in educational leadership from the University of Phoenix. Cara has worked in education, curriculum development, and teacher professional development for 20 years in preK-12 education and five years in higher education. She has experience supervising preK-12 adapted physical education, health education, and physical education in the largest Maryland school district. She is a board member for the Society of Health and Physical Education Maryland. She serves on the SHAPE America board of directors and as the chair for the Maryland State Department of Education's advisory council on health and physical education.

**Yvette Onofre** is an adjunct professor at Rowan University in the department of health and exercise science. She earned her bachelor of arts in sociology from the University at Albany–SUNY, her master of social work from Stony Brook University, and a master of exercise science and health promotion degree from the California University of Pennsylvania. She is currently a PhD student in language, literacy, and sociocultural education (urban education concentration) at Rowan University. Yvette received her holistic health coach training from the Institute for Integrative Nutrition and is certified as a corporate wellness specialist with the Corporate Health and Wellness Association. She has led nutrition talks at children's sports and fitness events, places of worship, senior centers, and health centers. She has worked with children, teens, adults, and families to help them reach physical goals, promoting psychological well-being and personal growth.

**Tiffany Monique Quash** is the qualitative/survey research methodologist with the Center for Teaching, Research and Learning at American University. She earned her PhD in leisure behavior from Indiana University's School of Public Health with a minor in higher education. Her research focuses on the experiences of Black womxn collegiate swimmers, the historical and intersectional understanding of race, gender, leisure, and swimming, and water competency programming at historically Black colleges and universities (HBCUs). In 2019, she delivered a TEDx Talks, "Learning to Swim is a Human Right," which is solution-focused to addressing the racial drowning disparity while celebrating the success of Black womxn swimmers. Dr. Quash is an avid swimmer and was a head swim coach for several teams in California. She currently resides in Virginia with her wife, Tasha, and their pet turtle, Leo.

# About SHAPE America

**SHAPE America - Society of Health and Physical Educators** serves as the voice for 200,000+ health and physical education professionals across the United States. The organization's extensive community includes a diverse membership of health and physical educators, as well as advocates, supporters, and 50+ state affiliate organizations.

Since its founding in 1885, the organization has defined excellence in physical education. For decades, SHAPE America's National Standards for K-12 Physical Education have served as the foundation for well-designed physical education programs across the country. Additionally, the organization helped develop and owns the National Health Education Standards.

SHAPE America provides programs, resources and advocacy that support an inclusive, active and healthier school culture, and the organization's newest program—health. moves. minds.®—helps teachers and schools incorporate social and emotional learning so students can thrive physically and emotionally.

## Our Vision

A nation where all children are prepared to lead healthy, physically active lives.

## Our Mission

To advance professional practice and promote research related to health and physical education, physical activity, dance and sport.

To learn more, visit **www.shapeamerica.org**.